P9-CLO-068

Sermons and Outlines
for Special Occasions

Sermons and Outlines

for

Special Occasions

by

JAMES STALKER, HENRY P. LIDDON,
DAVID JAMES BURRELL, AND OTHERS

ς ?

BAKER BOOK HOUSE
Grand Rapids 6, Michigan
1955

COPYRIGHT, 1952 BY
BAKER BOOK HOUSE

All rights reserved. No part of this book may be reproduced in any form without permission in writing from the publisher, except brief quotations used in connection with reviews in a magazine or newspaper.

First Printing, May 1952
Second Printing, June 1953
Third Printing, June 1955

Printed in the United States of America

PREFACE

This volume is another in the *Minister's Handbook Series*. It is preceded by SERMONS AND OUTLINES ON THE LORD'S SUPPER and FUNERAL SERMONS AND OUTLINES.

This book is a handbook for use in preparing sermons and addresses for special occasions. It includes complete sermons, condensed sermons, outlines, illustrations, quotations, poetry, and suggested sermon themes and texts.

The selections offered in this handbook are gleaned from the sermon masters and writers of yesteryears. Every minister will find this volume to be a rich source of usable material.

—The Publishers

CONTENTS

I. NEW YEAR'S DAY

Our Guide

JAMES STALKER

Thou shalt guide me with thy counsel, and afterward receive me to glory. — Ps. 73:24.

WE are met this morning to wish one another a happy New Year, and let me wish you one and all a happy New Year. It is a good thing surely that we should begin the year with prayer, seeking to lay our life anew on God's altar; and it is good also, I think, to begin it in Church, that our sympathies may not be confined within our own breasts, but be taught to circle round our friends and our fellow-members, and round the things and Kingdom of Christ. Now I like to give a New Year's day motto for the year, and it is often very delightful for me to find far on in the year that the New Year's motto is well remembered. I heard one of our elders, just a couple of months ago, quoting up at the mission last New Year's motto, and I am not sure but he quoted those of several years past. Now I am going to give you one to-day that I think will be very encouraging and helpful. You will find it in the Psalms—seventy-third Psalm, twenty-fourth verse: "Thou shalt guide me with thy counsel, and afterward receive me to glory."

I. "Thou shalt *guide me.*" The Word of God says a great deal about guiding. There are many prayers in it in which God's people ask for guidance, and there are many promises in it which God undertakes to guide His people. Now what does that imply? Who are they who need to be guided? Well, children do. When very young you know how a mother requires to take a child's hand, and even teach it to walk, and in many respects we are children. Some of us have just begun the Christian life, and even those of us who have been longer in it are in many respects children. You remember when Jeremiah was called to be a prophet, how he said at once, "Ah, God, I am a child"; and when

9

Solomon was called to be king, he said very much the same thing. Now when we think of our high vocation—for the Christian calling is both a prophetic, and a kingly and priestly vocation—we also say, "I am a child." We need to be guided.

Then, again, strangers need to be guided. When we are in a foreign land we need to take a guide-book with us. When we are in a strange town we need to ask our way. Now every new year as it comes is a foreign country. We have not passed this way heretofore. We do not know what the year contains. There are none who need guidance so much as the blind, and we may almost say that, as regards the future, we are blind. There is a dark curtain hanging before us, and we cannot penetrate the future, therefore we need some one to guide us.

Then, again, guidance is needed when any one's road is very adventurous or perilous. You know when travelers go away to Switzerland, and want to ascend the Alps, they have to take guides with them; and I believe that when the ascent is very perilous they are tied to the guide. Even that is not sometimes a perfect protection, because the guide may slip away; but if we are tied to our Guide, there is no fear that He will fail us. And our path is generally a perilous one. We are not going the broad highway of ordinary life; we are seeking the white heights of purity, the lofty heights of meditation and contemplation; and, therefore, we need a Guide to take us up the perilous and difficult way. And then, once more, the erring need a guide; and I think the most pathetic thought suggested by the words, "Thou shalt guide me," is how much we have gone astray in years past. There was a clear path, but how often we have turned to the right hand or to the left, and we know what the result of that has been, how disastrous both to us and to others; and when we remember our past errors, most pathetically and most earnestly of all do we say, "Thou shalt guide me."

II. "Thou shalt guide me *with thy counsel.*" There is, I am certain, an unconscious guidance in Providence. God sees us past many a peril that we do not see. There is a lovely phrase somewhere—I think it is in the Psalms—about guidance. It says, "I will guide thee with mine eye." What does that mean? It always makes me think of a mother, out in the open air, perhaps, sitting on a green, or in a room sitting with her charge; and her child is playing through the house, and she is sewing or knitting, but with the corner of her eye she is watching the little one all the time, and with her feet she pushes something out of the way to clear its path; or if she sees something sharp lying in the path she takes it quietly away. And I have no doubt unconsciously to us God thus guides us with His eye, taking many a perilous thing out of our path, shutting up many a by-way, controlling us often when we do not know it by His Providence, so that we are guided aright.

But on the whole the guidance of Christians by God is a conscious guidance. "I will guide thee with my counsel." It is an intelligent guidance. We come to think God's thoughts about our life. It is a voluntary guidance. He does not lead us against our will, but he makes our will insensibly to harmonize with His, and, therefore, He guides us with His counsel. Where do we find that counsel? Well, we find it now that we are gathered here to speak about guidance for the year. If we want really to be guided we must be searching the Word during the year more than ever we have done, more carefully than we have done. You that have any experience of this are aware how the Word throws light on every day's duties, and how the new difficulties and dangers of the way grow light by the Word of God. Another way in which He guides us by His counsel is by the preaching of the Word. And I would say to you who want to be guided, attend diligently upon the preaching of God's Word in His House. I think you can say that the sermon of the Sabbath day throws light upon the week, and your experience through the week often gives a wonderful meaning to the sermon. And then, last of all, God gives us His counsel through His Holy Spirit—by the Word, by preaching, and by the Spirit.

III. "Thou shalt guide me with thy counsel, and *afterward* . . ." Do you know I think that is the best word in the whole verse. It is a perilous way, it is a difficult way we are going on, but there is a glorious afterward. There is an afterward even for this world, and there is a glorious afterward for the next world. Now, my dear people, I think there is nothing laid on my heart so much to say to you this morning as this—do not despair in yourselves. Do not think that your life has come to an end, that you have already seen the best of existence. No; the best is still in front. I think that is a glorious hope to the Christian. In regard to the merely natural life there comes a time when everything begins to give way. The body gets stiff, and begins to fail. Even the memory begins to be lost, and the mind is not so reliable as it once was. The tabernacle has to be taken down, but it is not so with the inner life, the life of the spirit. Though the outward man perish, the inner man is renewed day by day. Do not despair of yourself, but keep a bright hope for the future.

Some of us have been reading dear Dr. Bonar's life during the last few days. Well, it is a very beautiful book in many ways, but I think Dr. Bonar's life—to me, at all events—had its greatest charm and best lesson in this: *that he never gave up*. He never thought that his service to God was done, and he never thought that God's goodness to him was done. He was ripening and growing to the very end. And can we not say this—I felt it whenever I came to Glasgow—that that dear old man's very presence in Glasgow streets was a message and a sermon? We all felt here that merely to have him there was might, a tower of strength to religion, and an encouragement to us all. And I would say to you who are growing old, look for an influence of that kind. Even though part of your activity has to cease, and some great scheme in which you have been engaged has to be laid aside, God has new forms of interest and activity for you. Do not look upon your life as done and over. I think, perhaps, we are far too apt to think our life is over. We soon begin to despair, and we do so in regard to the inner life. I dare say there is some one here who has been fighting hard with some sin or temptation, and you are beginning to despair. Don't despair! God will give you the victory yet. Perhaps some of you have been thinking, when you looked upon an advanced Christian, "I never could become like that. There is a beauty, a godliness that I never can attain." There is no beauty of holiness God cannot give you and me. Keep looking to the future. There is always an *afterward*. We have not exhausted Christ yet. We have not exhausted God's grace yet. The well of salvation is still deep and flowing. Look ever to the afterward.

And then there is the afterward of the next world, to which the text, perhaps, specially refers. "Thou shalt guide me with thy counsel, and *afterward receive me to glory*." I was saying a short time ago—I forget whether in the pulpit or the prayer-meeting—that one of the peculiarities of our time is the growing faith in the religious importance of the present life, but along with that there goes too much the want of interest in the future life. Now, I think, while we lay hold of the one we should take care and not lose the other. There was a time in the history of Christianity, an age in Europe, when the next world, so to speak, engrossed this world; the light of the coming glory so dazzled men's eyes they could not see the importance of time; and so they fled from common life and hid themselves in monasteries and nunneries. Well, we have got over that, but perhaps we have got too much over that. I think we have recovered a great truth of Christianity, a great thought of Christ, in taking this world very seriously, in looking upon it as a matter of great importance.

There is a great work to do here in the present life; there is a vast deal we have to do for ourselves and others and God, and we cannot, perhaps, make too much of it. Yes; but while we grasp that truth which Christianity at one stage lost hold of, don't let us lose hold of the other truth—the glory that is to come. Of course, it is possible to cherish that as a very idle hope, and I suppose it is from that the reaction has come. Heaven has been spoken about in an unnatural way, and therefore by degrees people have come not to care about it at all. Ah, but it is capable of doing two things for you. You remember what St. John said: "Now are we the sons of God, and it doth not yet appear what we shall be; but we know that, when he shall appear, we shall be like him: for we shall see him as he is." Therefore he adds: "And every man that hath this hope in him purifieth himself, even as he is pure." If the thought of Heaven has that effect on us, if it makes us purify ourselves that we may be fit for that exaltation, if the sense that we are citizens of that glorious country lays on us an obligation that leads us to live up to the dignity of the sons of God, then that is no idle or useless hope.

Then there is another practical issue, for the thought of heaven and its glory makes us wish to take others there. Oh, when we see what men are living for, when we see how unhappy the most of them are, do you not feel the passion in your soul to try to take some of them to Heaven with you? I have often said, both in public and in private, one of my chief ambitions for this congregation is that it may consist of those who are not only going to Heaven themselves, but trying to take a great many others with them; and if the thought of Heaven has that effect on us, it will be by no means an idle or impracticable thought.

Let me go over these points again. *"Thou shalt guide me."* We need guidance for all the reasons I mentioned. *"With thy counsel"*; there is not only an unconscious guidance, but an intelligent, voluntary guidance; and *"afterward"* — there is a glorious afterward for Christian hearts; first, the afterward of this world, and second, the afterward of the eternal world.

RESOLUTIONS, SHATTERED (Luke 15:18)

I. It is well to make good resolutions at this time.

II. We should be very careful in making our resolutions.

III. We should hold tenaciously to our determination no matter what it costs.

IV. How to be able to keep our resolutions.

V. The best resolution for an unconverted person to make.

— ANONYMOUS.

(SERMON THEMES AND TEXTS)

1. A Worthy New Year's Resolution, "As for me and my house, we will serve the Lord" (Josh. 24:15).
2. A New Opportunity, "Ye have not passed this way heretofore" (Josh. 3:4).
3. Constancy amid Change, "Thou art the same, and thy years shall have no end" (Ps. 107:27).
4. A Pleasant Prospect for the New Year, "My presence will go with thee" (Ex. 33:14).

BEGINNING OF THE NEW YEAR

There once was a very beautiful custom in Germany, which it would be well to imitate everywhere. On the first day of the New Year, whatever might have been the quarrels or estrangement between friends and relatives, mutual visits were interchanged, kindly greetings given and received — all was forgotten and forgiven. Let this custom begin with reconciliation to God, then friendship and fellowship may be found that shall be blessed and lasting. — BEECHER.

> I asked the New Year for some message sweet,
> Some rule of life with which to guide my feet;
> I asked, and paused: he answered soft and low,
>   "God's will to know."

"Will knowledge then suffice, New Year?" I cried:
And, ere the question into silence died,
The answer came, "Nay, but remember, too,
     God's will to do."

Once more I asked, "Is there no more to tell?"
And once again the answer sweetly fell,
"Yes! this thing, all other things above:
     God's will to love."

                     — Anonymous.

NEW YEAR THOUGHT

I would be quiet, Lord,
   Nor tease nor fret;
Not one small need of mine
   Wilt Thou forget.

             — Julia C. R. Dorr.

II. PALM SUNDAY

The King Comes to his Capital

T. WHITELAW

John 12:12-16

I. *The King's Person. Jesus.*
1. Recently condemned by the Sanhedrin.
2. Who had tacitly claimed to be Zion's King.
3. Who had repeatedly proved His right to this dignity, and lately established it by the miracle at Bethany.
4. Who now asserted it in the most open and unambiguous manner by riding in royal state into His capital.

II. *The King's Credentials.*
1. Consisted in the fact that He was coming to His metropolis in the name of the Lord. He was no usurper, but One to whom the throne belonged by Divine appointment. The crown pertained to Him in a more real sense than to any of Israel's kings.
2. Were displayed in the manner of His coming. He came exactly as predicted. Had He come as kings of the earth are wont to approach their capitals—as Solomon and His successors — on fiery chargers, there would have been required no further demonstration that He was not God's Messiah. He came in humility and righteousness—indisputable tokens of His claim.

III. *The King's Welcome.*
1. The multitudes — accompanying, meeting.
2. Their homage — waving palms and strewing garments in the way.
3. Their acclaim — "Hosannah."

IV. *The King's Attendants.* The Disciples.
1. Ignorant at the time of its significance; perhaps imagining the present realization of their earthly hopes.
2. Afterwards alive to its spiritual and eternal meaning.

V. *The King's Enemies.* The Pharisees. The spectacle seemed for a moment to confound their plots. It filled them with indignation, urged them to recrimination, made them more determined. Caiaphas' prophecy appeared on the eve of coming true. The nation was slipping from their hands.

Lessons:

1. The religious instincts of the multitudes.
2. The credibility of ancient Scripture.
3. The illumination Christ's glorification has cast on history.
4. The certainty that the world will ultimately be won by Christ.

How Are We to Become A Part of That Great and Joyous Palm Sunday Procession

J. A. SEISS

Matthew 21:1-9

1. *First of all, we must recognize in Jesus our divine Lord and Saviour.* It is under this conviction and belief that the whole procession moves. Its leadership, its center, its joy, its inspiration, is "He who cometh in the name of the Lord." And until we learn to know, appreciate, and honor Him as the meek and glorious King of Salvation, our place is not in that happy throng.

2. *Furthermore, our hearts must be attuned to the excellent son of these people.* ZACHARIAS led off in it when he said, "Blessed be the Lord God of Israel; for He hath visited and redeemed his people, and hath raised up a horn of salvation for us in the house of his servant David." The aged SIMEON re-echoed it when he sang, "Lord, now lettest thou thy servant depart in peace, according to thy word; for mine eyes have seen thy salvation." MARY voiced it, saying, "My soul doth magnify the Lord, and my spirit hath rejoiced in God my saviour." PAUL struck the grand keynote of it when He exclaimed, "Thanks be to God, which giveth us the victory through our Lord Jesus Christ." And all the myriad hosts gathering around the sacred altar have never ceased to sing it, as with angels and archangels, and all the company of heaven, they praise and magnify the glorious Name of the Eternal, saying, "Hosanna in the highest! Blessed is He

that cometh in the name of the Lord." And only as we learn that song, and keep it living in our hearts and on our tongues, are we of that blessed company, moving on with the King, to live and reign with Him in the City of God.

How is it then with you, dear friends? Have you learned to recognize and honor your rightful King and only Saviour? There are professed Christians who make more of a brutal game than of a divine sacrament. Is that a following of Jesus? There are people who are louder and heartier in their praises and laudations of victors in trials of muscle and carnal contests, than over Him who conquered death and hell and opened for them the Kingdom of heaven. Is this a following of Jesus? O, the follies and hallucinations of people who fain would count themselves the children of God! But to all the meek and forbearing the King comes once more, offering to be their Saviour and everlasting Friend. He comes with free forgiveness and eternal life for every one who will receive Him. Open then your hearts and homes that He may enter. Receive Him, that He may cast out all alien powers, and become your everlasting Lord and Benefactor.

(SERMON THEMES AND TEXTS)

1. The Triumphal Entry, "Rejoice greatly, O Daughter of Jerusalem: behold thy King cometh unto thee" (Zech. 9:9).

2. Who is This? "And when he was come into Jerusalem, all the city was moved, saying, Who is this?" (Matt. 21:10).

3. Christ Enthroned, "Yet have I set my King upon my holy hill of Zion" (Ps. 2:6).

4. Homage to the King, "And they that went before, and they that followed, cried saying, 'Blessed is he that cometh in the name of the Lord: Blessed be the kingdom . . .'" (Mark 11:9, 10).

THE PRESENT VISION

The triumphal procession of Christ is still going on. Already it numbers countless millions, who, as these people cast their garments before Jesus as He rode in triumph, have cast their talents, their money, their time, all that they possess, before Him, to aid His cause, and hasten His success.

> "Ride on triumphantly; behold, we lay
> Our lusts and proud wills in Thy way."
>
> — SCHAUFFLER.

PALM BRANCHES

> O'er all the way green palms and flowers gay
> Are strewn this day in festal preparation;
> Where Jesus comes to wipe our tears away;
> E'en now the throng to welcome Him prepare.

Refrain

> Join all and sing, His name declare,
> Let every voice resound with acclamation,
> Hosanna! Glory to God!
> Praise Him who cometh to bring us salvation!

> His word goes forth, and peoples by its might
> Once more regain freedom from degradation:
> Humanity doth give to each his right,
> While those in darkness find restored the light.

> Sing and rejoice, O blest Jerusalem,
> Of all thy sons sing the emancipation,
> Through boundless love; the Christ of Bethlehem
> Bring faith and hope to thee forevermore.
>
> — AUTHOR UNKNOWN.

III. GOOD FRIDAY

The Crucifixion

F. W. FARRAR

There they crucified him, and the malefactors, one on the right hand, and the other on the left. — Luke 23:33.

On these great solemn days of the church, sermons are the least needful. The day itself preaches to us. Its lessons, its services, its memories are so many sermons; and every Sunday of the year helps to explain and to emphasize the lessons of those great facts of which Christmas Day, Good Friday, and Easter Day are special memorials. Eighteen and a half centuries have flowed back into the dark abyss of time since that first Good Friday, yet how fully does the fourfold narrative of the Gospels enable us to call up the most memorable event in the world's history! A turbulent afternoon in spring, an execution, a surging crowd, the eve of a great annual festival which has brought thousands to Jerusalem, the dim, unconscious sense of some great crisis and tragedy, rocks tremulous with earthquake, a sky darkening with preternatural eclipse! Stand amid that vile, promiscuous crowd; what is the spectacle which has summoned them together? There are three crosses on Golgotha; on the right hand and on the left are two robbers, crucified for murder and rebellion; on the central cross, with its mocking title of scorn over His head in three languages, "This is the King of the Jews," with women weeping at His feet as though their hearts would break, hangs a sinless Sufferer, One who had lived as never man lived, One who spake as never man spake, One who had loved His brethren as never man had loved before! Guilt and innocence are alike nailed upon those crosses; redeeming Godhead and ruined humanity hang tortured there; and that Sufferer was the Saviour of mankind.

Now, those three crosses symbolize two opposite, two eternal, conflicting facts—they are the signs of an *awful defeat,* and

21

of *an unutterable victory;* they are the proof of *an* appalling misery and of an irresistible, triumphant hope.

I. *The Awful Defeat.*

Gaze at which cross you will, you will see in it the fall, the degradation, the utter corruption of humanity, the acme, the zenith, the triumph— and at this moment it might have seemed the final triumph — of the enemy of souls. Death itself, death at the best, is full of awe; death even when the mute, beseeching appeal of every glance is anticipated by love, when every pang is soothed, every tear is wiped away with the touch of consummate tenderness; death even when prayers and hymns are uttered softly by the dying bed, and children's faces look upon it, and every eye is wet with tears!

But death like this! Death in the cruelest and vilest form which has ever been invented even by the base and cruel East; a death of ghastly and lingering torture, which even cruel nations, brutalized by despotism, and inured to blood, regarded as the supreme form of all that was miserable and execrable! And this death, inflicted in slow, horrible agonies, and the devilish inventiveness of torture by man upon his brother man when he is in the full flush and prime of his life! Death when the living man, who was made to be "but little lower than the angels," in the supreme moment of his destiny is loaded with nameless insult, and hounded out of the world with fiendish execration! Does not the mind shudder at it! Does it not look like the enthronement of the most hideous and malignant of the principalities of evil over the life of man? From what other source could spring these frightful insults against the majesty of manhood, against the awfulness of death? Said not our Lord Himself, "This is your hour and the power of darkness"?

And does not the voiceless horror become yet more horrible when we think that on these three crosses hang those who represent alike the loftiest and the lowest humanity — represent manhood taken up into Godhead, and manhood degraded into demonhood — represent guilt, innocence, repentance, ending their lives in the same dire anguish, under that darkening sky, in the common horror of the tragedy of apparent failure too awful for any human imagination to conceive?

1. For *guilt was there, and guilt is the darkest problem which this world knows.*

That impenitent robber, perhaps a follower of Barabbas, familiar with who knows what scenes of blood and plunder, with who can tell what scenes riding like a nightmare on his breast, does he not represent the horror of the door of finished crime? Yes, he was a criminal; but no criminal was always a criminal; no man is made in a moment a votary of vice. The first step toward the ruined man is inconstancy of mind and lack of faith in God. "First cometh to the mind a bare thought of the evil, then the strong imagination of it, then delight and evil motion and full consent; and so, little by little, our wicked enemy getteth complete entrance for that he is not resisted in the beginning.

That wretch, that impenitent murderer, in his agony, was once a prattling child, and some proud young Hebrew mother had bent over his cradle, and parted his dark hair, and guided his pattering footsteps, and folded his little hands to pray. Little by little, through slow, invisible gradations of degeneracy, inch by inch, step by step, from carelessness to vice, from vice to sin, from sin to crime, he had sunk to this. Sin had triumphed in his mortal body and over his immortal. The powers which war against man's soul had gained over that man so dread a mastery that even here and now, on the cross, he can blaspheme and perish in his evil courses, and go to his own place. The death of an impenitent criminal by the hands of his brother man on the cross, or on the scaffold, is the grimmest and ghastliest of grim and ghastly tragedy. Let us drop the curtain over it. No ray of light can pierce that midnight, save such as shines unseen by us behind the veil.

And that other robber, the penitent, what good there must have been once in him if his faith could leap like a dying flame out of these white embers of his life! We know not whether the legend of him be true, that in youth, when he was a robber, he had spared the Virgin Mother and her Child in the flight to Egypt; but in him, even more than in the other, we see the shipwreck of fair hopes, the ruin of faculties created for heavenly ends, the growth of sins unresisted, the rushing avalanche of final ruin which overwhelms those sins! The remission of sins is not the remission of their consequences; the penalty of violated law must be paid even by the penitent, and paid to the uttermost farthing.

2. *And between those two hangs on the cross the Perfect Man, the Sinless Sufferer.* On the white robes of His divine humanity

there has never been a stain; over the blue heaven of His holiness there had never floated even the shadow of a cloud. He had been all love, all wisdom, all innocence. He had been the Word become flesh, He who clothed Himself "with light as with a garment, and spreadeth out the heavens like a curtain" had been content to dwell in a tent like ourselves, and of the same material — had come down from the starry heights of heaven, amid angels' songs, to live through a sweet infancy, a gracious boyhood, and a winning youth of humble obscurity — to us a divine example to show us the Father, the All-purity, All-tenderness, All-compassion, to heal the leper, to open the eyes of the blind, to go about doing good, to release the tortured soul of the demoniac, to preach the Gospel to the poor, to undo the heavy burden, and let the oppressed go free.

And thus He had lived, and thus the world rewarded Him! For lies and baseness, for selfish greed and destructive ambition, for guilty wealth and mean compliance, the world has a diadem; for perfect holiness it has the cross! The darkness quenched the Light, His own disowned Him. They had repaid by hatred that life of love; envy, malice, slander, calumny, false witness, had done its work. Jesus had been excommunicated, hunted as a fugitive, with a price upon His head, buffeted, insulted, spit upon, mocked, scourged, crowned with thorns — thus had the world shown its gratitude to its Redeemer; and the end was here! After thirty hours of sleepless agony Jesus was hanging upon the cross. Infinite malignity! Could there be any greater proof of man's ruin than the fact that this was the sole reward which was requited to immeasurable love?

3. And *the mass of mankind, too, the mass of ordinary, average humanity at its lowest, was represented in that scene* — the common herd and scum, and low, coarse, average of humanity in all ranks. The stream of humanity in its muddiest vileness was following under those kingly and closing eyes. I think an ignorant, obscene mob of godless men, mere fevers of lust, and leprosies of uncleanness, and ferocities of brutal rage, is of all sights the one which makes one shudder most. It is a multitudinous infamy of baseness, stupidity, and savagery. This crowd was a sink of the dregs of many nations. The Roman soldier was there, coarse and cruel and ignorant and corrupt; drinking, gambling, swearing at the foot of the cross; the Jew of many nations was there, narrow, fanatical, a chaos of relentless hatreds; the supple, unclean

Greek was there, from all the corrupted shores and cities of Asia and Africa; and the hoarse murmur of their jeers and blasphemies, in which even the crucified wretches beside Him joined, mingled themselves with the sobs of those poor Galilean peasant women in His dying ears! The King of men: and this is what manhood had become! And yet the divine love can still love on unashamed in the face of the enormities which wronged it.

4. And, saddest of all, *there was religion there — what called* itself religion, believed itself to be religion, was taken for religion *by the world;* and the corruption and perversion of religion is almost viler and more perilous than godlessness when religion has sunk into mere callous conventionalism and mere irreligious hypocrisy. A city which they called the Holy City lay before Him, white, beautiful, vocal with religious songs, busy with festive preparation, but its heart defiled with blood, and a band of invincible darkness lying across its radiant sunlight. The elders, who should have taught the people, had been the deadliest in their yells of "Not this man, but Barabbas!" The Pharisees, who made the greatest pretense of being the sole representatives of the Orthodox Church, passed by Him, a band of self-deceivers, wagging their heads, and taunting with jeers His awful agony. The priests, who slew the victims, who burnt the incense, who trod the golden Temple courts, they had been the worst of His enemies, the most active of His murderers! What shall be done in the world when its very religion had become irreligious, when its very baptisms need baptizing, when it has sunk into a mass of usurping ambition, human ordinances, deceiving illusions, and historic lies? Guilt itself is a less hopeless spectacle than religion which has no love and no truth in it. What shall we think of priest and Pharisees who crucified the Lord of Glory? Yet the most dreadful fact of all history is that the church, or what calls itself the church, what vaunteth itself as the only church, and anathematized and excommunicated all other religious bodies, has ever been at deadlier enmity with God's prophets even than the world, and has chanted its loudest hallelujahs over St. Bartholomew massacres and the ashes of slaughtered saints.

And now the Holy City was using the secular arm of heathen Rome, and religion was firmer even than irreligion in murdering the Son of God. Well might earth groan and tremble and fiends rejoice!

"It was their hour, and the power of darkness."
Thou palsied earth, with noon-day night all spread;
Thou sickening sun, so dim, so dark, so red;
Ye hovering ghosts that throng the starless air,
Why shakes the earth, why fades the light? Declare
Are those His limbs, with ruthless scourges torn?
His brows all bleeding with the twisted thorn?
His the pale form, the meek, forgiving eye,
Raided from the cross in patient agony?
Be dark, thou sun; thou noon-day night, arise
And hide: oh, hide! that dreadful sacrifice!

II. *The Unutterable Victory.*

And so came the end. Seven times only in brief sentences He had broken His kingly silence — once to pray for His murderers; once to promise Paradise to true repentance; once in human tenderness to His mother; one brief cry of spiritual desolation; one single word, the only word recorded in the four Gospels, the one word of physical anguish, "I thirst;" one loving, trustful prayer; then the one victorious, triumphant, divinely-exultant word, "It is finished." Finished was His holy life; with His life, His struggle, His work; with His work, the redemption; with the redemption, the foundations of the new world. Over the world, rulers of this darkness, here intensified, here concentrated, Christ had triumphed for ever and ever more.

For, thank God, there is the other side of this great and terrible day of the Lord.

1. If it was the hour and power of darkness, *it was also the hour and power of infinite deliverance.* If it was the proof of an appalling ruin, it was also the pledge of an illimitable hope, for we know that the cross, which looked like the uttermost victory of Satan, bruised the head of Satan, and that the seeming victory of death was the rending from death of its shameful sting.

Nothing is further from the way in which Christ's apostles and Christ Himself teach us to regard the cross than the morbid, effeminate, gloating luxury of self-stimulated emotion. The unnatural self-torture of the flagellant, the hysterics of the convulsionary, the iron courage of the mistaken penitents, are manifestly out of place in contemplating that cross; which is the symbol of sin defeated, of sorrow transmuted, of effort victorious; which is the pledge of God's peace with man, and man's peace with God; which is the symbol of divine charity on fields of slaughter; which was the banner in the van of every battle which good has waged with ill! The cross does not mean weeping, anguish, morbid wailing, morose despair; it means joy, it means peace, it means exultation, it means the atonement, it means the redemption, it means the liberty of humanity, it means the advance of holiness, it means the remission of sins!

Nothing is more futile than to merge ourselves in a sort of luxury of imaginative and artificial woe over the physical sufferings of Christ. There is not one word in the whole New Testament to encourage such worship. Christ is not suffering now; He is not now upon the cross; He is among heaven's eternal glories and infinite beatitudes. He is not now the crucified; He is not now the dead, not now the absent, not now the humiliated; but, as has been truly said, He is the Incarnate, the Present, the Living, the Prince of Peace on earth, the everlasting King in Heaven! What His life is, what His commandments are, what His judgments will be, these He impresses on us — not only what He once did, or what He once suffered. And what He now requires of us is what He is now doing; that is, the pure, joyful, beautiful practise of primitive and unperverted Christianity. And the fall from that faith and all the corruptions of its abortive practise, may be summed up briefly as habitual and too exclusive contemplation of Christ's death instead of His life, and the substitution of His past sufferings for our present duty.

2. *It was a tremendous sacrifice;* never let us forget that! Let it bring home to our hearts, with infinite sense of shame, the exceeding sinfulness of sin. It is for that, and not for Christ, that we are called upon to mourn. Better even the crude fanaticism of the Jogi or the Dervish, better the self-immolating rapture of the wretches who flung themselves under the car of Juggernaut, than the insolent self-satisfaction of liars and adulterers and slanderers who yet dare to be terribly at ease in Zion! Let us never forget how much it cost to redeem our souls, how exceeding must have been the sinfulness of that sin which needed such a sacrifice; yet let us, at the same time, bless God beside the cross that if no plummet can sound the abyss of human degradation, neither is there any instrument which can measure the altitude of God's love! "I saw," said George Fox, "that there was an ocean of death and darkness, but an infinite ocean of light and love flowed over the ocean of darkness, and in that I saw the infinite love of God."

For he must be blind, indeed, who does not recognize what the cross has done. You may judge of its effects by this, that when Christ died He left but a timid and miserable handful of disappointed Galilean followers, terrified, helpless, infinitely discouraged — and that now, nearly nineteen centuries after His death, we see the two immense proofs of His divinity, historically in all that we mean by Christianity and in all that we mean by belief that there is forgiveness in God; so that "if any man sinneth we have an advocate with the Father, Jesus Christ the righteous, and he is the propitiation for our sins; and not for ours only, but also for the sins of the whole world."

3. Nor, lastly, is this all. *If one arm of the cross points, as it were, to infinite forgiveness, the other points to illimitable hope.* Truly, we need it still! Life is still a dark and stormy sea, strewn with innumerable shipwrecks, and its restless water still casts up mire and diret . . . As far as the world is concerned God's saints may still have cause to cry in age after age, "How long, O Lord, how long?" but as far as each human soul is concerned, it may, in Christ, escape from evil and doubt and misery and death, "as a bird out of the snare of the fowler," and find by experience the fruition of the eternal promise, "Thou shalt keep him in perfect peace whose mind is stayed on thee." For because Christ died, and liveth forevermore, access is ever open to the foot of the Throne of Grace, mercy is unfailing to the cry of penitence, grace is inexhaustible to the servant who offers himself wholly for the Master's use.

Darkness and earthquake, the shame and anguish of Good Friday, are but the prelude to the bursting dawn and glorious spring of Easter! By the cross we, too, are crucified with Christ; but alive in Christ. We are no more rebels, but servants; no more servants, but sons! "Let it be counted folly," says Hooker, "or fury, or frenzy, or whatever else; it is our wisdom and our comfort. We care for no knowledge in the world but this, that man hath sinned, and that God hath suffered; that God has made Himself the Son of Man, and that men are made the righteousness of God!"

CHRIST'S COMPLETED WORK (John 19:30)

What was the purpose of Christ's mission on earth?

1. He came on earth to declare and reveal to men the will of God.

2. He came also to be our example.
3. He came to earth to make atonement for sin.
— ALBERT LEE.

(SERMON THEMES AND TEXTS)

1. A Voluntary Sacrifice, "The cup which my Father hath given me, shall I not drink of it" (John 18:11).
2. A Vicarious Death, "Surely he hath borne our griefs and carried our sorrows" (Isa. 53:4).
3. Mission Completed, "It is finished" (John 19:30).
4. Rejecting the Christ, "They cried, Crucify him! Crucify him!" (John 19:10).

THE BENEFITS OF HIS DEATH ARE INEXHAUSTIBLE.

The passion of our Lord is like a great river flowing down from a mountain, which is never exhausted. — VIANNEY.

PRE-EMINENCE OF THE CRUCIFIXION

If you have not yet found out that Christ crucified is the foundation of the whole volume, you have read your Bible hitherto to very little profit. Your religion is a heaven without a sun, an arch without a keystone, a compass without a needle, a clock without spring or weights, a lamp without oil. It will not comfort you. It will not deliver your soul from hell. — RYLE.

UNDER THE CROSS

Oppressed with noonday's scorching heat,
    To yonder cross I flee;
Beneath its shelter take my seat;
    No shade like this for me!

Beneath that cross clear waters burst,
    A fountain sparkling free;
And there I quench my desert thirst;
    No spring like this for me!

A stranger here, I pitch my tent
    Beneath this spreading tree;
Here shall my pilgrim life be spent;
    No home like this for me!

For burdened ones a resting-place
  Beside that cross I see;
Here I cast off my weariness;
  No rest like this for me!

            — HORATIUS BONAR.

BEFORE THE CROSS

Sweet the moments, rich in blessing,
Which before the cross we spend;
Life, and health, and peace possessing,
From the sinner's dying Friend.

Truly blessed is this station,
Low before His Cross to lie,
While we see divine compassion,
Beaming in His gracious eye.

Love and grief our hearts dividing,
With our tears His feet we bathe;
Constant will, in faith abiding,
Life deriving from His death.

For thy sorrows we adore Thee,
For the pains that wrought our peace,
Gracious Savior! we implore Thee
In our souls Thy love increase.

Here we feel our sins forgiven
While upon the Lamb we gaze;
And our thoughts are all of heaven,
And our lips o'erflow with praise.

Still in ceaseless contemplation,
Fix our hearts and eyes on Thee,
Till we taste Thy full salvation,
And, unvailed, Thy glories see.

            — JAMES ALLEN

IV. EASTER

Has Christ Risen?

HENRY P. LIDDON

It is the Spirit that beareth witness — I JOHN 5:7.

WITHOUT faith in the resurrection of Jesus Christ serious Christianity is impossible; when the resurrection is denied, apostolic doctrine and Christian faith are alike empty of their vital force, or, as the apostle says, "are vain"; a Christ who died and never rose from death is not the Christ of the New Testament. He is not the Christ of Christendom; a Christ such as this would never have converted the world, and the Christianity, so to call it, which centers in such a Christ as this will not long even interest it. A Christ who dies, but who never has conquered death, is plainly an intellectual makeshift. He is a creation and the toy of souls who are passing, whether consciously or not, from the faith of their fathers to infidelity. If it can be shown that Christ did not really rise from His grave, Christianity sinks at once to the level of a purely human theory of life and conduct whose author altogether failed to make good His language to Himself. Certainly His religion has played too great a part in human affairs to be forgotten by history. But it would, in the event contemplated, have forfeited all right to obtrude itself any longer on the attention of mankind as God's last and greatest revelation of Himself to His rational creatures.

It is natural to ask What is the evidence that Christ really did rise from the dead? And here, as St. John says in this epistle, "It is the Spirit that beareth witness." St. John, indeed, is speaking immediately of that faith in our Lord's eternal Sonship which overcomes the world; but since the resurrection is the main proof of our Lord's divinity, since He was declared to be "the Son of God with power" as regards His higher, holy nature by the resurrection from the dead, it follows that the Spirit must also bear witness, in some sense of the word, to the resurrection.

31

And He does this in two ways. It is His work that the historic proofs of the resurrection which have to come down to us, and which have addressed themselves directly to our natural reasoning faculties have been marshaled, recognized, preserved, transmitted in the Church of Christ. The Spirit, as we Christians believe, bears witness in the sacred pages of the New Testament to the resurrection of Jesus; but He also bears another witness, as we shall presently see in His action, not so much on the intelligence as on the will of a Christian believer.

I. Let us ask ourselves, first of all, What is the evidence with which we are supplied on the subject of the resurrection — what is there to be said on the subject to a person who believes — I will not say in the supernatural inspiration, but in the general trustworthiness of the writings of the first Christians.

A. In order to know that our Lord did really rise from the dead we have to satisfy ourselves that three distinct questions may be answered.

1. Of these the first is this: *Did Jesus Christ really die upon the cross?* For, if He merely fainted or swooned away, then there was no resurrection from death; then He merely recovered consciousness after an interval. The Evangelists, each one of them, say expressly that He did die; and the wonder is, not that He died when He did after the three hours agony on the cross, but with all His sufferings at the hands of the soldiers and of the populace before His crucifixion — with all these sufferings He should have lived so long. But suppose that what looked like death on the cross was merely a fainting fit, would He have survived the wounds in His side inflicted by the soldier's lance, through which the blood yet remaining in His heart escaped? We are expressly told that the soldiers did not break His limbs and that He was already dead, and before Pilate would allow His body to be taken down from the cross he ascertained from the centurions in the land that He was already dead.

But, suppose again, against all this evidence, that when He was taken down from the cross He was living, then He must have been suffocated by Joseph of Arimathea, and Nicodemus when they embalmed Him. They rubbed a hundred pounds weight of myrrh and aloes over the surface of His body, and then they bound bandages tightly around each of His limbs, and His head, and His body before they laid Him in the grave. The Jews carefully inspected and sealed the tomb; they had sentinels placed there; they were satisfied that the work was thoroughly done. To do them justice, the Jews have never denied the reality of our Lord's death; it is impossible to do so without a paradox.

2. The second question is this: *Did the disciples take our Lord's dead body out of the sepulcher?* They would not have wished to do it; why should they? What could have been their motive?

Imagine yourselves, my brethren, in the position of the disciples when convinced of the reality of our Savior's death. They either believed in His approaching resurrection, or they did not. If they did believe it, they would have shrunk from disturbing His grave as an act not less unnecessary than profane; if they did not believe in it, what must have been their estimate of their dead Master? They must now have thought of Him as of one who deceived them, or was Himself deceived. If He was not a clever impostor who had failed, he was a sincere but feeble character, who had Himself been the victim of a religious delusion.

On either supposition, why should they arouse the anger of the Jews and incur the danger of swift and heavy punishment? What would have been gained by persuading the Jews under those circumstances that He had risen, or that He was the Messiah, or that His anticipations had come to pass, if all the while they themselves knew that He was dead and that His body had only been shifted by themselves from one resting-place to another? If they were religious adventurers, they could not have hoped to succeed. The attempt would have been no less fruitless than absurd. The world, after all, is not converted to a new religion by sleight of hand; and in order to believe that the apostles would not have wished to remove our Lord's body from the sepulcher, it is only necessary to credit them with ordinary common sense. But had they wished they surely could not have dared it. Until Pentecost they were, by their own account, timid men. When Jesus was arrested all the disciples "forsook him and fled." St. Peter denied Him; only St. John ventured to follow Christ to Calvary, to stand near the cross. When our Lord stood in the midst of the council chamber they took Him for a phantom; they were seized with terror. Were these the men to risk a desperate struggle with the guard of soldiers and to take a dead body out of its tomb at the dead of night? Even if one or two of the disciples would have ventured on such an enterprise, could they have counted on the cooperation of the others?

And, once more had they desired and dared to remove our Lord's body from its grave, such a feat was obviously beyond their power. The tomb was guarded by soldiers; every precaution had been taken by the Jews to make it secure. The great stone at the entrance could not have been rolled away without much disturbance, even if the body could have been removed without attracting attention. The character of the guards themselves was at stake. Had they countenanced or permitted any such crime their almost inevitable detection would have been followed by severe punishment. Certainly, the guard at the sepulcher was bribed by the leading Jews to say that the body of Jesus had been taken away by the disciples while they slept. Whatever the eagerness of the soldiers might have been to touch the money, they would have been cautious in circulating such a report as this, and the Jews could not have ventured to treat it as practically true. When they imprisoned and scourged St. Peter and the other apostles, when they persecuted to death first St. Stephen and the other servants of Christ, they did not accuse their victims in any one instance of having stolen Christ's body from His grave and then circulating a false report of His resurrection. The charge was merely that they had preached the resurrection after having been ordered to be silent.

3. And a third question is the following: *What is the positive testimony that goes to show that Jesus Christ did rise from the dead?*

a. There is, first of all, the witness of all the apostles. They affirmed publicly that during forty days they saw Jesus Christ alive; that they had conversed with Him; that they ate and drank with Him; that they touched Him. They gave their lives in attestation of this fact. Their conduct after the day of Pentecost is that of men whose trustworthiness and sincerity of purpose are beyond dispute. You and I, my brethren, unless we were strengthened by Divine grace, might too, probably, hesitate to give our lives for what we knew to be undoubted religious truth; but, at least, we would not make any considerable sacrifice for the sake of impressing the world with the truth of an occurrence which we believed in our hearts to be very doubtful.

b. Next, there is the testimony of a large number of persons besides the apostles. Take the case of the three thousand con-

verts of St. Peter's first sermon on the day of Pentecost. Here
were three thousand people professing belief in the resurrection
fifty days after the date of the occurrence. They had every
means of verifying its truth or falsehood. They were on the
spot; they could decide the time; they could collect and investi-
gate the current stories; they could take them from the Jews;
they could cross-question the guards; they could compare; they
could analyze the conflicting opinions flitting around them; they
had unrivaled opportunities of satisfying themselves as to its
truth or falsehood; and at the risk of comfort, nay, of life, they
publicly professed their belief in its truth. They could not be
Christians without making this profession; they had no hesita-
tion about making it.

Or, consider the case of the two hundred and fifty or more persons still living when St. Paul wrote his first Epistle to the Corinthians — persons who had seen the risen Jesus. On one single
occasion during the forty days after that He was seen of about
"five hundred brethren at once, of whom the greater part re-
main until this present, but some are fallen asleep." There is no
doubt about the document containing this assertion. The most
destructive of the negative schools of modern criticism ranks
this first Epistle to the Corinthians among the four books of the
New Testament whose genuineness and authenticity it still holds
to be beyond dispute. There is no reason for questioning the ac-
curacy of the apostle's information; and the significance of the
statement in history could not be exaggerated. Five hundred
persons could not be simultaneously deceived. Their testimony
would be considered decisive as to any ordinary occurrence,
when men wished only to ascertain this simple truth.

B. *And the force of this flood of testimony is not really weak-
ened by objections which did not, you will observe, directly chal-
lenge it; but which turn on accessory or subordinate points.*

1. For instance, *it is said that the evangelical accounts of the
resurrection itself, and of our Lord's subsequent appearance,
are difficult to reconcile with each other.* At first sight they are,
but only on first sight. In order to reconcile them, two things
are necessary; first, patience; and, secondly, determination to
exclude everything from the narrative which does not lie in the
texts of the Gospels. Two-thirds of the supposed difficulties
are created by the imagination of the negative commentators.
Left to themselves, the evangelists do not, indeed, tell us a great
deal that we would really like to know; but, at least they do not

contradict each other. If they had forged the whole story, and had written with any degree of concert, they would have been at once more explicit and less careless about appearances than they are; they would have described Jesus bursting forth visibly from the grave in a blaze of splendor, terrifying His guards, welcoming His faithful followers, who would have been collected on the spot. As it is, these are just what might be expected in four narratives of the same event, written at different periods, by different authors, who had distinct sources of information at command. Each says what he has to say with blunt and simple directness, without any eye to the statement of the others, or to the possible comments of the hostile critics.

To show their agreement in detail would of course, carry me far beyond our limit; suffice it now to say, that in describing the resurrection, as elsewhere, so here, Scripture takes no precautions against hostile judges. Scripture speaks as might a perfectly truthful child in a court of justice, conscious only of its integrity, and leaving the test, whether criticism or apology, of what it says, entirely to others. It proceeds on the strong conviction that in the end, in this, as in other matters, wisdom is justified of her true children.

2. *It is further objected, that the resurrection was not sufficiently public.* Jesus, it appears ought to have left His grave in the sight of a crowd of lookers-on, and when risen, He ought to have hastened to show Himself to the persons least likely to believe in His resurrection — to the Jews at large, to the high priest, to Pilate, to His executioners; even, it is of late hinted, to a scientific commission of some kind, which might have first investigated, and then drawn up a report upon the subject. Had He appeared to the Jews, would they, think you, have believed Him? Would they not have denied His identity, or else argued that a devil had taken His form before their eyes, just as before they had dared to ascribe His miracles to Beelzebub?

There was no greater reason for our Lord showing Himself to the unbelievers of that day than for His showing Himself to the unbelievers of each succeeding century from then until now. They who cried on the day of Calvary, "Let him come down from the cross and we will believe him," would not really have believed Him if He had taken them at their word. Unbelief is the product of a particular state of heart and mind; much more than that, it is the product of an absence of a particular sort of evidence. The Jews had ample opportunity of ascertaining that the resurrection was a fact if they had desired to do so; but, as it was, they were not in a mood to be convinced even by the evidence of their senses. It was with them as with the brethren of the rich man in the parable — "If they hear not Moses and the prophets, neither will they be persuaded though one rose from the dead." If the testimony of the apostles and of so many other persons was insufficient, the appearance of the risen Lord Himself would not have done more than add to the list of their rejected opportunities, and so add to their condemnation.

3. *Far deeper than these objections is that which lies against all miracles whatever* as being at variance with that conception of a rigid uniformity in the processes of nature which is one of the intellectual fashions of our time; suffice it to say that any idea of natural law which is held to make a miracle impossible is also inconsistent with intelligent belief in the existence of God. When a believer in God talks of a law of nature he can never mean more than God's uniform mode of working in a particular instance. He cannot mean anything that is independent of God, any force or impact, which, if originally coming from God, has now acquired a right to maintain itself in spite of Him, or is, at any rate, somehow out of His reach. To hold this idea of the law of nature is to hold that God is not Master of the universe — in other words, that He is not Himself. The only real question for the serious believer in God is whether the producible evidence for an alleged miracle is sufficient.

II. Here, then, we are coming round to the point from which we started; for it is natural to ask, *"Why, if the resurrection can be proved by evidence so generally sufficient, was it at the time, and is it still, rejected by a great many intelligent men?"* The answer to this natural and legitimate question will be of practical importance to all of us. There can, I apprehend, my dear brethren, be no sort of doubt that, if an ordinary historical occurrence is attested as clearly as the resurrection of our Lord all the world would believe it as a matter of course. Nay, more: if an extraordinary occurrence traversing the usual operations of God in nature were similarly tested, it would be easily believed if only it stood alone as an isolated wonder connected with no religious claims, implying no religious duties, appealing only to the bare understanding, and having no bearing, however remote, upon the will.

The reason why the resurrection was not always believed upon the evidence of those who were witness to it was because to believe means for a consistent and thoughtful man to believe in and accept practically a great deal else. To believe the resurrection is to believe implicitly in the Christian faith. The divine Person of our Lord, the atoning work of our Lord, the teaching authority of our Lord, the efficacy of His perpetual intercession in heaven, and of the great means of grace He has given us on earth, depend on and are bound up with His resurrection.

If the intellect alone could have the decision of the question in its keeping, the number of unbelievers would be comparatively small. The real difficulties of belief lie, generally speaking, with the will; and nothing is more certain — I may add nothing is more alarming — than the power of the will to shape, to check, to promote, to control conviction. For the will, too, has reasoning power, so to call it, of its own; the will is, in a sense, a second reason within us. It looks ahead, does the will; it watches the proceedings of the understanding with jealous scrutiny; it watches, and, if need be, it interferes. It sees the understanding on the point of embracing a conviction; which means it knows very much more than speculative assent; which means action or suffering, that is to say, something entirely within its own province — the province of the will. It sees the conviction all but accepted; it sees the understanding stretching out its arms, as it were, to welcome the advancing truth, and it mutters to itself, "This must not be, or I shall be compromised; I shall have to do or to endure what I do not like." And such is the power of the will, the sovereign faculty in the human soul, that it can give effect to this decision. It can baulk and thwart the straightforward action of the intellect; it can give it a perverse twist: it can even set it thinking actively how best to discredit and refute the truth which but now it was on the point of accepting.

And this is what happened to the Jews of the Pentecost period. Those Jews had no prejudices against miracles; on the contrary, they expected miracles to occur from time to time. They entirely believed in the astonishing miracles in their own past history. Had it been for them only a speculative question, they would have believed in the resurrection, too; but, so far from being a speculative question only, it was charged with practical consequences. The will of the Jew instinctively suggested to him, "If Jesus of Nazareth rose from His grave, then a great deal will follow for which I am not prepared. Then He is the Messiah, then the present order of things will be seriously changed; new duties, new sacrifices, will be expected of me and mine. I must see if His resurrection is so very certain, if there is not some natural explanation of it to be found, if it is not due to a trick or to a hallucination; anyhow, it must not and it cannot be accepted as true. It may triumph at the bar of probable evidence. Granted; but common-sense, as I understand common-sense, is against it." This is something like what the Jew would have thought to himself, and his will would have carried the day against his understanding.

And thus we may understand what it is that the Spirit does to produce faith. He does not set aside or extinguish the operations of the natural reason; but He does change by His merciful and wonderworking touch the temper, the direction of the will; and thus He sets the reason free to do some sort of justice to the evidence before it. It is thus within us that the "Spirit beareth witness." The evidence of the resurrection is of such a character that an unspiritual man with no more than average powers to understand the value of a probable, as distinct from a mathematical argument, can at once see its strength and force. But this perception is useless unless the will be ready to do its part, or, at least, not to interfere with the verdict of the intellect. And it is the Spirit which secures this. The evidence for the resurrection was not stronger on the day of Pentecost itself than it was on the day before; but the descent of the Spirit made all the difference — made it possible for the three thousand converts to do the evidence some sort of justice.

And we can see, too, why it is that St. Paul makes so much of faith, especially faith in a living Christ, in all his great epistles. Faith is for him not merely the assent of the understanding; it is also the assent of the will. It is even less an intellectual than a moral act. This is one reason why it justifies. In a true act of faith the whole moral nature of man concurs in the justifying assent that is given to the revealed truth. If the understanding were alone concerned, there would be no more reason for our being justified by faith in a crucified and living Christ than for our being justified by faith in the conclusions of a problem in Euclid. It is because the will must endorse the verdict of the understanding, and so must mean obedience as well as mental assent, that "by grace ye are saved, and that not of yourselves, it is the gift of God."

Pray, dear brethren, for the divine and eternal Spirit, who witnesses to the resurrection, as in the sacred books of Scripture, so by His action upon hearts and wills of men. Remember

there is no man that can say that Jesus is the Lord but by the Holy Ghost; so no man can profess, to any purpose, faith in Christ's resurrection but by the Holy Ghost. "It is the Spirit that beareth witness" now, as nineteen centuries ago, by that influence on the will of man which leaves the intellect at liberty to do justice to the evidence before it. Pray that most blessed Spirit so to teach your hearts and wills that you may, at least, have no reason for wishing the resurrection to be untrue. Pray Him for His gracious assistance that you may recover or may strengthen the great grace of faith and have your part in the blessed promise of the apostle: "If thou shalt confess with thy mouth the Lord Jesus, and shalt believe in thy heart that God hath raised him from the dead, thou shalt be saved."
(Adopted)

CHRIST'S RESURRECTION THE TYPE OF OURS
(Rom. 6:4)

The sons of Zarephath, Shunem, and Nain were brought back from the dead, as were Lazarus and Eutychus, but these did not share in the resurrection. Their bodies were not changed from corruptible to incorruptible, from mortal to immortal; they were still death's prisoners on parole. But over the risen body of Christ or His disciple, death has no power. Enoch and Elijah were "translated," "changed," like those who are alive at Christ's coming again; mortality was swallowed up of life.

Christ is the first-born of the dead; and His resurrection shows the law and method of ours. The points of resemblance we may indicate.

I. *He rose, as we shall, by the power of the Holy Spirit.* In each period of His life He was dependent upon the Spirit; and the same Spirit who had nestled to His heart in His baptism hovered over the grave in Joseph's garden; and on the third day loosed the pains of death, because it was not possible He should be holden of it. The Holy Spirit forgets no body which has been made His temple. He shall "quicken our mortal bodies."

II. *His resurrection was unobtrusive,* like all divine work; like the unfolding of flowers. The doors of our tombs will open on noiseless hinges; the fetters will drop lightly from our hands; our bodies will rise into immortal beauty like a dream.

III. *His resurrection was leisurely.* The burial-clothes were folded and laid aside, as Christ without haste rose in majesty.

God's children shall not go out by flight, for the Lord has gone before them, and His glory shall be their reward.

IV. *His resurrection was irresistible.* When Joseph and Nicodemus left Him in the tomb, the guards tried to hold Him fast, But God said, and will say for us: "Let my people go."

V. *His risen body was like His mortal body.* As in the buried seed, the principle of vitality was unchanged. His glorious body was different from the body of His humiliation, yet it was the same. He could vanish and pass through doors, yet they knew Him the same. So those that sleep in Jesus become fairer, stronger, swifter, more apt for service, yet wake with the endeared features, familiar tones, and happy companionship.

VI. *What Christ does in renewing our souls He will yet do in renewing our bodies.* This will be the top-stone in the edifice of redemption.

— F. B. MEYER.

CHRIST'S RESURRECTION THE PROMISE AND PROPHECY OF OUR OWN (I Cor. 15:20)

On this glorious morn, amid these flowers, I give you an Easter greeting.

I find in the text a prophecy of our own resurrection. Before I finish I hope to pass through every cemetery and drop a flower of hope on the tombs of all who have died in Christ. Rejoicing in Christ's resurrection we rejoice in the resurrection of all the good.

The greatest of all conquerors is not Alexander, or Caesar, or Napoleon, but death. His throne is in the sepulcher. But his scepter shall be broken, for the dead in Christ shall arise.

There are mysteries around this resurrection of the body which I can't explain. Who can unravel the mysteries of nature? Who can explain how this vast variety of flowers have come from seeds which look so nearly alike? Tell me how God can turn the chariot of His omnipotence on a rose leaf? Mystery meets us at every turn.

Objects one: The body may be scattered — an arm in Africa, a leg in Europe, the rest of the body here. How will it be gathered on the resurrection morn?

Another objects: The body changes, perishing continually. The blood-vessels are canals along which the breadstuff is conveyed to the wasted and hungry parts of our bodies. Says another: A man dies; plants take up parts of the body: animals eat the plants, and other men eat the animals. Now to which body will belong these particles of matter?

Are these all the questions you can ask? If not, ask on. I do not pretend to answer them. I fall back on these words, "All that are in their graves shall come forth."

There are some things, however, we do know about the resurrected body.

1. *It will be a glorious body.* The body, as we now see it, is but a skeleton to what it would have been were it not marred by sin.

2. *It will be an immortal body.*

3. *It will be a powerful body* — unconquerable for evermore — never tired.

May God fill you to-day with glorious anticipations! Oh, blessed hope!

— T. DeWitt Talmage.

(SERMON THEMES AND TEXTS)

1. Christ the First Fruits, "Now is Christ risen from the dead and become the first-fruits of them that slept" (I Cor. 15:20).
2. Joy Born of Easter, "And they departed quickly from the tomb with fear and great joy" (Matt. 28:8).
3. An Attestation of the Divinity of Christ, "And declared to be the Son of God with power, according to the spirit of holiness, by the resurrection from the dead" (Rom. 1:4).
4. Death Vanquished, "Who hath abolished death, and brought life and immortality to light through the gospel (II Tim. 1:10).

EMBLEM OF THE RESURRECTION OF CHRIST

But as the sun, when to us it is set, begins a new day in another part of the world, so Christ, having finished His course in this world, rises again, and that to perform another glorious part of His work in the world above. — Flavel.

THE RESURRECTION A PLEDGE

His resurrection is a pledge, not merely an illustration, of the resurrection of mankind. He is the first fruits, as represented

in Scripture; they are the harvest. He is the forerunner: they
are the company for which He goes forth to make preparation.
— BEECHER.

Come, ye saints, look here and wonder,
    See the place where Jesus lay;
He has burst His bands asunder;
    He has borne our sins away;
        Joyful tidings,
    Yes, the Lord has risen to-day.
                            — THOMAS KELLY.

In the bonds of Death He lay
    Who for our offence was slain;
But the Lord is risen to-day,
    Christ hath brought us life again,
Wherefore let us all rejoice,
Singing loud, with cheerful voice,
        Hallelujah!
                        — MARTIN LUTHER.

LIKE EASTER LILIES
Like Easter lilies, pure and white,
Make Thou our hearts, O Lord of Light!
Like Easter lilies, let them be
Sweet chalices of love to Thee!
                        — EMMA C. DOWD.

V. ASCENSION DAY

The Ascension of Christ

CHARLES SIMEON

Luke 24:50-53

Our blessed Lord, having accomplished all that was necessary to be done on earth, led His disciples out "as far as to Bethany," and went up from the midst of them to heaven, giving them ocular demonstration that His removal from them was such as He had taught them to expect: "I came forth from the Father, and am come into the world; again, I leave the world, and go to the father" (John 16:28). In this text we notice two things:

I. OUR LORD'S DEPARTURE FROM HIS DISCIPLES.

"Having loved his own which were in the world, he loved them unto the end" (John 13:1); and He expressed His love to them most particularly in the very instance of His departure: "He lifted up his hands, and blessed them"; and it was in this very act that He was taken up from them: "While he blessed them, he was parted from them." His removal in the midst of this act ought not to be passed over as a mere accidental and uninteresting occurrence. It surely may be considered as intimating to us two things:

A. *What was His Object in Coming Into the World?*

The apostle Peter tells us that God sent Him "to bless you, in turning away everyone of you from his iniquities" (Acts 3:26). Man was cursed as a transgressor of God's law; nor could he, by any means remove the curse, or obtain any blessings whatever. Sin interposed an insurmountable obstacle in his way. But Jesus undertook to remove this obstacle; to expiate the guilt of sin by the sacrifice of Himself, and thus to open a way for man's reconciliation with his God. This sacrifice He had now offered, and had finished the work which God had given Him to do (John 17:4).

45

Now, therefore, He authoritatively pronounced His disciples blessed: blessed, as believing in His name; blessed, as interested in His death; blessed, as committed to His protection; and blessed, as fellow-heirs of His glory. Just as the high-priest, after offering his sacrifice, was to bless the people (Lev. 9:22), so now Jesus intimated that His work of redemption was completed, and that He, as our great High-priest was empowered to bless His people with all spiritual and eternal blessings (Gen. 14:18; Eph. 1:3).

B. *What Should Be His Occupation When He Was Departed from the World?*

He was not now going to relinquish His concern for His own. On the contrary, He would still be as mindful of them as ever. He was going to heaven to prepare a place for them (John 14:2); to make continual intercession for them (Heb. 7:25); to take on Himself the management of the universe for them, and to receive a fulness of all gifts and graces for them, that they might receive out of it according to their several necessities.

His removal, though it interrupted the sight of His person, and the hearing of His voice, should not interrupt the communication of His blessings; and, if we look to Him with the eye of faith, we may behold Him, as it were, at this very instant occupied as He was at the moment of His departure from the world. He is still blessing His believing people; yea, He will yet further extend His favors to the remotest corners of the earth, for "men shall be blessed in him: all nations shall call him blessed" (Ps. 72:17).

II. The Effect It Produced Upon His Disciples.

When our Lord had told them of His intended departure, they were sorrowful (John 16:20); but now that He was really gone, they were altogether full of joy. They were now better instructed in the nature of His kingdom than they had been before. Indeed, even to the last they retained some expectation of a temporal kingdom (Acts 1:6-7); but His departure from them dissipated that delusion, and taught them to look up to Him for far greater blessings.

Now, the effect which was produced in *them* by the *sight* of His ascension, ought equally to be wrought in *us* by the *recollection* of it; and I shall have addressed you to no purpose, if you do not depart from this place with a measure of those very feelings with which the apostles were impressed on this occasion. I call upon you therefore now:

A. *To Adore Him.* He is worthy of all adoration. Notice that, "they worshipped him." "All men should honour the Son, even as they honour the Father" (John 5:23). Let us then adore Him as our incarnate God and Saviour.

B. *To Rejoice in Him.* Who can contemplate Him seated on His throne of glory, and constituted "the head over all things to the church" (Eph. 1:22), and not rejoice in Him? Such joy is characteristic of His people (Phil. 3:3); and it ought to be as elevated and as fervent, as our feeble nature will admit of (1 Pet. 1:8). The disciples "returned to Jerusalem with great joy."

C. *To Consecrate Yourselves to Him.* The apostles from this time appear to have given themselves up wholly to the exercises of devotion. As far as relates to the affections of the soul, we must consecrate ourselves as entirely to God as they. "Ye are bought with a price: therefore glorify God in your body, and in your spirit, which are God's (I Cor. 6:20). Let us serve Him in his Church at the appointed seasons of public worship, and also in our closets, where no eye sees us, but His.

D. *To Wait for the Accomplishment of All His Promises.* At Jerusalem the disciples waited in expectation of the promised Power from on high. The Lord has also given us "exceeding great and precious promises" (II Pet. 1:4), comprehending everything that we can desire for body and soul, for time and eternity. In due time Jesus will come again from heaven in like manner as He ascended thither; and then will that last promise be fulfilled: "I will come again, and receive you unto myself; that where I am, there ye may be also" (John 14:3). O, that in the meantime He may find us with our loins girt, and our lights burning, and ourselves "like unto men that wait for their lord" (Luke 12: 35-36).

LESSONS FROM THE ASCENSION (Luke 24:51)

1. Since our Lord has ascended we are never to think of Him as dead.

(a) He stands in heaven today the living head of His redeemed Church.

(b) He stands in heaven today our priestly advocate.

(c) He stands in heaven today as the controller of all things in God's providential government.

2. Since our Lord has ascended we are never to think of Him as distant.

3. Since our Lord has ascended we are never to think of Him as different.

— HOMILETIC REVIEW.

(SERMON THEMES AND TEXTS)

1. The Lord's Attitude in the Ascension, "While he blessed them, he was parted from them, and carried up into heaven" (Luke 24:51).
2. The Expediency of the Ascension, "It is expedient for you that I go away" (John 16:7).
3. The Forerunner, "I go to prepare a place for you" (John 14:2).
4. The Comfort of the Ascension, "Go to my brethren, and say unto them, I ascend unto my Father, and your Father; and to my God, and your God" (John 20:17).

THE ASCENDED CHRIST, OUR INTERCESSOR

Once, I suddenly opened the door of my mother's room, and saw her on her knees beside her chair, and heard her speak my name in prayer. I quickly and quietly withdrew, with a feeling of awe and reverence in my heart. Soon I went away from home to school, then to college, then into life's sterner duties. But I never forgot that one glimpse of my mother at prayer, nor the one word — my name — which I heard her utter. Well did I know that what I had seen that day was but a glimpse of what was going on every day in that sacred closet of prayer, and the consciousness strengthened me a thousand times in duty, in danger, and in struggle. When death came, at length, and sealed those lips, the sorest sense of loss that I felt was the knowledge that no more would my mother be praying for me. In John 17 we hear Christ praying for us — just once, a few sentences; but we know that this is only a sample of the intercession for us that goes on forever. Nothing shall interrupt this pleading, for He ever liveth to intercede.

— J. R. MILLER.

FEELING KINSHIP

Christ's life here assures us of His kinship with us on earth; His ascension enables us to feel our kinship with Him in heaven. Earth is not more lonely because of His return, but heaven becomes more clearly the home to which our hearts are to turn. He went before in order to welcome us when we are summoned to follow. But for the present struggle of life, also, His ascension has its significance.

— A. W. KELLY.

ASCENSION OF CHRIST

As Joseph was secretly sent before by God's intendment to prepare a place in Egypt for his brethren; so more openly doth Christ ascend to heaven, professedly declaring that to be His business, "I go to prepare a place for you."

— GOODWIN.

HAIL THE DAY

Hail the day that sees Him rise,
Ravished from our wishful eyes!
Christ, awhile to mortals given,
Re-ascends His native heaven.

Him the highest heaven receives,
Still He loves the earth He leaves:
Tho returning to His throne,
Still He calls mankind His own.

Lord, tho parted from our sight,
High above yon azure height,
Grant our hearts may thither rise,
Following Thee beyond the skies.

— CHARLES WESLEY.

VI. MOTHER'S DAY

5/12/51
a.a.

The Shunammite's Son

II Kings 4:18-37

I. A PROUD MOTHER'S DELIGHT.

1. Her *son*. She took pleasure in watching his childhood and growth, etc. He was her treasure.

2. He was *her only son*. This would increase her anxiety and also her delight in him (Judg. 11:34; Luke 9:38).

3. The *child of promise* (verses 16, 17). Hebrew wives were anxious to have children — especially to have a son. This desire is natural and not confined to Hebrews. Her husband was well off, and here was a son to inherit the father's property and name.

Harvest time comes. Her child is sent out to play in the harvest field. She watches him depart, and thinks of the happy day he will have, and the meeting at night.

II. A TENDER MOTHER'S TRIAL.

The child is in the field, engaged in youthful sports. He is playing at harvesting. Then comes the sunstroke. "My head! my head!" The father sorrowfully orders, "Carry him to his mother." A mother is ever the best nurse.

The mother sees her child returning, not running by the father's side, but carried. Her anxiety! Her fears!

Tenderly she nurses her child. The time drags on, but the mother does not tire. The child dies, but she has faith left. Faith is a good companion in trouble. This child of promise could not be lost! So the mother carries the child into the prophet's chamber.

III. A GOOD WIFE'S EXAMPLE.

The wife and mother considers not her own feelings only, but her husband's also. She thinks of how great his grief will be on his return, and finding death in his house!

She resolves on immediate action. She will visit the man of God! She knows that she cannot do this without assistance, for the distance is very great. She prudently calculates the time, and concludes, that she can accomplish it before the day is over.

She hastens to the field and begs for one of the young men. Evidently she does not tell her husband. She would not grieve him. Here is a hint for those who unnecessarily burden other people with their troubles.

IV. A HAPPY MOTHER'S REWARD.

She returns with the prophet. This is a wonderful display of faith. Who would bring a doctor to a dead child? This faith is rewarded. The child is miraculously restored to life.

1. *The first reward.* She joyously clasps the living child to her heart.

2. *The second reward.* The father's return and greeting. He is pleased to find that the child is well. Picture his astonishment at learning the history of the day. Here is a lesson for our husbands and fathers. Men at their occupations little think of the trials at home. They should commend their dear ones to God.

3. *Her after-rewards.* The preservation and growth of this child. Only mothers can fully appreciate this reward.

Learn: —

1. *To appreciate and repay a mother's love and anxious care.*
2. *To bear your trial nobly without making other people bear it.*
3. *To realize that faith will be rewarded.*

— CLASS AND DESK (*Adapted*).

THE POWER OF A MOTHER'S INFLUENCE
II Chronicles 22:3

"For" is a kind of explanation, the reason assigned for results which are given. "For his mother was his counsellor to do wickedly."

I. *It begins early in life.*

Education begins sooner than parents imagine; long enough before they are responsible, even when they begin to see, feel, and observe. Hence: great importance to have first teaching of a child. Early impressions are elementary principles out of which mature life is organized. "When should I begin the education of my children now four years old?" asked a mother from a clergyman, who replied, "Madam, if you have not begun already you have lost those four years. From the first smile that gleams upon an infant's cheek your opportunity begins."

II. *It moulds through life.*

A living power, forming character and directing conduct. The child becomes a man, the subject becomes a sovereign; influence is thus repeated and transmitted. Home is the most powerful school in the world. A mother's influence for good or evil is mightier than pulpits and thrones. "My opinion is," said Napoleon, "that the future good or bad conduct of a child depends entirely on the mother."

III. *It leaves permanent impress upon life.*

Alexander the Great could never correct the faults of gait and manners learned in childhood from Leonidas, his master. The face, words, and example of mothers leave even more permanent influence. "Every first thing continues for ever with the child; the first color, the first music, the first flower, paint the foreground of his life. Every new educator effects less than his predecessor; until, at last, if we regard all life as an educational institute, a circumnavigator of the world is less influenced by all the nations he has seen than by his nurse."

> "The fond attachment to the well-known place,
> Whence first we started into life's long race,
> Retains its hold with such unfailing sway,
> We feel it e'en in age, and at our latest day."

(SERMON THEMES AND TEXTS)

1. A Mother's Influence, "When I call to remembrance the unfeigned faith that is in thee which dwelt first in thy grandmother Lois, and thy mother Eunice; and I am persuaded that in thee also" (II Tim. 1:5).

2. Joyful Parents, " . . . he that begetteth a wise child shall have joy of him. Thy father and thy mother shall be glad, and she that bare thee shall rejoice" (Prov. 23:24, 25).

3. The Way of a Mother, "But his mother kept these sayings and pondered them in her heart" (Luke 2:51).

4. The Depth of Folly, "A Foolish son despiseth his mother" (Prov. 15:20).

This was true in the life of Ahaziah. It is equally true today.
— Preacher's Homiletic Commentary (Funk and Wagnalls)

MOTHER, BREVITIES

The mother's heart is the child's schoolroom.

— BEECHER.

The future destiny of a child is always the work of the mother.
— NAPOLEON BONAPARTE.

MOTHER'S PRAYER

I cannot tell you how much I owe to the solemn words of my good mother. It was the custom on Sunday evenings while we were yet little children for her to stay at home with us, and then we sat around the table and read verse after verse and she explained the Scriptures to us. After that was done there came a time of pleading and the question was asked how long it would be before we would think about our state, how long before we would seek the Lord.

Then came a mother's prayer, and some of the words of our mother's prayer we shall never forget even when our hair is gray.   — CHARLES HADDON SPURGEON.

Love droops; youth fades;
The leaves of friendship fall;
A mother's love outlives them all.
—OLIVER WENDELL HOLMES.

No one knows of the work it makes
    To keep the home together;
Nobody knows the steps it takes,
    Nobody knows but Mother.
Nobody knows the lessons taught
    Of loving one another;
Nobody knows the patience sought,
    Nobody knows but Mother.

— SELECTED.

For the hand that rocks the cradle
Is the hand that rules the world.
— WILLIAM STEWART ROSS.

VII. MEMORIAL DAY

Memorials

J. HIGGINS

Joshua 4:1-9

Memorials! What are they? For what do they stand, and what do they teach? They are special signs of Divine interposition in human lives, and commemorate some event or circumstance claiming special remembrance and study. (Such is this day on which we commemorate a special event in the history of our nation.)

I. *This Memorial Was Commemorative and Suggestive.*

1. *It commemorated a new departure.* They had not been this way before, they had never stood so near the fulfilment of hope as they did now. This is typical of every life. We all have our new departures, times of marked and decisive change, when some sudden bend in the road completely changes the track, leads us into new scenes of activity or rest, giving us new revelations and new experiences, and are truly periods of deep interest, epochs, red-letter days in our lives; we cannot forget them, and have raised memorials marking them as points to be remembered and studied.

2. *It commemorated a signal mercy.* Every Christian life has its seasons of peculiar need, which are often made special means of grace. And should he not raise memorials to mark both the trial and the mercy?

3. *It commemorated a remarkable deliverance.* What a sublime spectacle! When all human aid is unavailing, and nothing can save but direct Divine intervention, then Jehovah commands the waters to stand up upon a heap, again showing His salvation to His people. Some such memorials you have in your life. Some time of pressing need, when human help failed, and God came to your deliverance by opening up a path through the deep waters for you. And have you made no mark, no sign, put up no lasting reminder?

II. *The Value of Such Memorials.*

1. *They witness for God.* They stand at different points on the ways of life, bearing silent but telling testimony to the power and grace of the Infinite Father in some time of sore and pressing need, confirming our faith in the doctrine of the conscious, abiding, personal presence of God in the lives of His people.

2. *They remind us of mercies received in the past.* We are consciously faulty in memory, are apt to forget the blessings already received, and to grow impatient and fretful when things are a little contrary; then it is of service to us to go back a little in our history to some of these times of God's special nearness to us, when He gave us such unmistakable proof of His presence and grace by some marked deliverance, some special blessing, or some signal answer to prayer; when we can refresh our faulty memories by putting our hand upon some place, or time, or event in our life that we had marked by a stone of memorial, as a record of faith in God and gratitude to Him.

3. *They inspire confidence and hope for the future.* Much was before them to perplex.

4. *They check despondency and gloom.*

5. *They supply precious lessons of Divine faithfulness.* God would have us raise these memorials by the way to remind us of His covenant engagements. The past shall repeat itself in our future.

6. *These memorials are of service to others.* The pillar at Gilgal was not only to be a memento of the sovereign mercy of God to those who had actually witnessed the cutting off of the waters of Jordan, but it was to supply to posterity some precious lessons of Divine majesty and love. Much so it is with the memorials of Christian lives — they exert a helping influence on other lives.

7. *These memorials supply incentives to increased devotion, and stimulate to loftier praise.* In this day of scepticism, coldness, indifference, and practical infidelity, when the actual presence of God in individual lives is more or less ignored, it is both refreshing and reassuring to take up Christian biography and hear how the holy men and women who have passed into the Father's house accounted for similar events in their lives. I have sometimes seen family Bibles marked with peculiar hieroglyphics which a stranger could not read or understand; but ask the husband or wife to tell you what these marks mean, and you find that each has a history precious and sweet to the marker. They

are pillars that have been raised to remind them of some special answer to prayer, when they pleaded that promise; or when some extraordinary light broke upon the mind, on a certain day, as they pondered and prayed over that verse; or perhaps it was a literal fulfilment of another promise on which they had rested in a time of distressing calamity, and they have placed these memorials there to call to mind the signal mercy of God in their time of urgent need, and they would as soon doubt the need as they would their source of supply. "God did it for us," they say, "as surely as He divided Jordan for Israel to pass over to Canaan." I have also heard matured Christian men converse together on God's dealings with them, and have felt a strange thrill pass through me as one of them has put his hand upon some pillar in his life and said, "Here God met me, and I communed with Him. It was a time of bitter pain and need, and I was bowed down to earth with the burden, and was fainting by the wayside, but the Lord drew very near, and I seemed to hear His voice speaking to me, and asking me to tell Him about the pain, and I was drawn out to tell Him all, and He blessed me there, by giving in a way marvellous to me just what I needed; I rose up a strong man, and the grace was so like a miracle that I put up this memorial, and this spot is very dear to me, for here I saw God face to face and my life is preserved."

STONES OF MEMORIAL (Josh. 4; 6:7).

I. The Memory of God's Goodness Is Honoring to God Himself.

II. The Memory of God's Goodness Is a Stimulus to Piety.

III. The Memory of God's Goodness Is an Encouragement in Time of Trial, Danger, and Fear.

(SERMON THEMES AND TEXTS)

1. The Day of Memory, "What mean ye by this service?" (Ex. 12:26).
2. A Nation's Tribute to Its Heroic Dead, "This day shall be unto you for a memorial" (Ex. 12:14).
3. War for the Sake of Peace, "Neither shall they learn war any more" (Isa. 2:4).
4. Our Debt to the Soldiers, "And the people said unto Saul, Shall Jonathan die, who hath brought this great salvation in Israel?" (I. Sam. 14:45).

MEMORIAL DAY REMINDERS

The supporters of religion gave their lives for a principle. These martyrs of patriotism gave their lives for an idea.

— SCHUYLER COLFAX.

DEAD, HONOR OUR PATRIOT

Memorial Day is consecrated to the soldiers; it is dedicated to patriotism; around this sacred day cluster precious memories of our fallen brave. Over the silent chambers of our sleeping comrades we wreathe garlands of flowers — symbols of our love and gratitude. These graves are the Nation's shrine, the Mecca to which patriots journey to renew their devotion to the cause for which these patriots died. The fruits of their victories are a united country. This is a sacred heritage purchased by their valor and sealed by their blood. History is their encomium. Battle-fields attest their courage.

"Sleep, heroes sleep;
Your deeds shall never die."

GOD OF OUR FATHERS, WHOSE ALMIGHTY HAND

God of our fathers, whose almighty hand
Leads forth in beauty all the starry band
Of shining worlds in splendor thro' the skies,
Our grateful songs before thy throne arise.

Thy love divine hath led us in the past,
In this free land by thee our lot is cast;
Be thou our ruler, guardian, guide and stay,
Thy word our law, thy paths our chosen way.

From war's alarms, from deadly pestilence,
Be thy strong arm our ever sure defense;
Thy true religion in our hearts increase,
Thy bounteous goodness nourish us in peace.

VIII. CHILDREN'S DAY

Timothy

J. R. MACDUFF

"To Timothy, my dearly-beloved son; Grace, mercy, and peace from God the Father, and Christ Jesus our Lord.

I thank God, whom I serve from my forefathers with pure conscience, that without ceasing I have remembrance of thee in my prayers night and day.

When I call to remembrance the unfeigned faith that is in thee, which dwelt first in thy grandmother Lois, and thy mother Eunice; and I am persuaded that in thee also." — 2 Tim. 1:2, 3, 5.

What a pleasant surprise it is to meet a lovely flower blooming in a desert!

Here is a description of such a flower found by the great Apostle Paul in the Highlands of Asia Minor — the Pagan city of Lystra.

Timothy ought to be specially interesting to you, my young friends, because we first meet him in sacred story, a little child playing round the feet of his mother and grandmother, Lois and Eunice. By them his lips were taught early to sing the praise of the God of Abraham and Isaac and Jacob, and his heart early to love the Holy Scriptures. It is supposed that his father had died when his son was in infancy, or at least before he came to boyhood.

His grandmother would doubtless say to him sometimes (as grandmothers say to their grandchildren still), "Come, dear child, on my knee. I will tell you stories from the sacred writings which you will love to hear." You may believe, too, he would, just like you, have his favorite Bible stories: perhaps Noah in the Ark, or Israel crossing the Red Sea, or God delivering His own laws from the top of Mount Sinai amid thunders and lightnings, or David playing on his harp in the valleys of Bethlehem, while feeding his father's sheep. Before he went to bed, we can think of him clasping his little hands together, thanking God for all His mercies. And then, when he was asleep and the curtains of night were drawn around him, his mother and grandmother would kneel by the side of his couch, and ask the Great and Good Shepherd of Israel who never slumbers nor sleeps, to bless their boy.

Or, when Sabbath morning came round, he would in all likelihood accompany them, along with any other pious Jews who may have dwelt in that heathen city, to some peaceful spot near the town, perhaps into some quiet wood, or by some "riverside" (as in the case of Lydia: Acts 16:14), "where prayer was wont to be made." There they would read together the Old Testament Scriptures; imploring the love and guidance and protection of the God of their fathers; and beseeching Him speedily to send the Great Messiah promised to their Nation, in whom not Israel alone, but all the families of the earth were to be blessed.

The prayers, both public and private, of these two devout women for their darling child were heard and answered in a way they never dreamt of: for he became in due time an honoured servant of the divine Redeemer. The little Jewish boy of that Lystrian home, turned out a standard-bearer in the first Christian army: — a polished corner-stone in the rising Christian Temple: and now, wherever the Gospel is preached in the whole world, his name is known and his memory loved!

Blessed are those children who have such a mother and such a grandmother as Timothy had! My young friends, be grateful to God if He has given you such a gift. Well has it been said that "the Church owes specially much to the glorious company of Christian *mothers*." I am sure no heavenly lessons will ever cling to you like those you received from their lips. The experience of the well-known John Newton, in his slave ship, is that of many, however the circumstances may vary. He was brought to his knees in sorrow for his sins and became a converted man, when, one dark night standing by the helm of his vessel, he thought of a hymn his dear mother had taught him!

Remember if God has given you this great blessing of a good father or mother or pious relatives, you will have all the more to answer for at the Judgment day, if you are forgetful of their holy lessons and example. Think how different your case is, compared with that of thousands of ragged, neglected children in the streets, who have never been taught to kneel down in prayer, or to read their Bible, or to enter church; who have never had the pattern of a good life set before them which Timothy had; who have never, it may be, heard of the name of God, save in dreadful oaths. Remember the words of the Lord Jesus how He said, "To whom much is given, from them will the more be required" (Luke 11:48).

As years went on, Timothy grew up from being a child and a little boy, to be a youth. St. Paul, as the first great Christian missionary, was going from place to place carrying the good news of the Gospel. One day he was proclaiming his Master's name in the town of Lystra, where I have told you Timothy lived. There was a Temple at its gates, where sacrifices were offered to Jupiter, whom the heathen inhabitants called "the King of Gods and men." They considered him the Protector of their city, and did not at all like strangers coming among them in order to lead them away to the worship of another God. The idolatrous Lystrians, therefore, were greatly offended at the Apostle's preaching. They stoned him in the open street, and he was dragged away outside the walls, and left there half dead.

Timothy (now about fifteen years old) was very probably one of those who looked upon that cruel scene. He never forgot it. No! he could not banish from his mind the sight of that bold, brave man, who risked dear life and all he had, for the sake of the truth as it is in Jesus. He could not fail to keep in sacred remembrance, the meek, calm, patient spirit he showed towards those who had done all they could to murder him. Indeed it has been thought, and it is far from unlikely, — that it was to the home of Eunice and Lois that the poor bleeding Apostle was borne. I do not think, with his sores and wounds, that Paul could have had much sleep that night: all the more so, as it was needful for him, before dawn of morning, to escape out of the city in case the angry mob might assail him once more. A further beautiful idea has been suggested, — that the young boy may have sat by the midnight lamp at the side of that couch of anguish, whispering or repeating to his future "father in the faith" some of those gracious sayings he had himself been taught from the Word of God; perhaps from the parchment roll which contained the Psalms of David — or some of the comforting utterances of the Great Isaiah.

At all events, from that hour the soul of Timothy seems to have been knit to St. Paul, as we read in the Old Testament of Jonathan's soul being knit to David; and he became what the Apostle loves afterwards to call him — "Timothy, my own son." St. Paul was not only brave, but good; he trusted in God and had always the one thought in his mind to do what was right. Timothy read this "living Epistle." He read his goodness just as plainly as you would read the writing of a letter or the printed words of a book. He became, from that day, "a good soldier of Jesus Christ." From that time too, onwards, it is delightful to watch these two loving servants of their gracious Lord. They were very different in many ways. The one was young and the other was in middle-age: — the one, I think, was naturally timid — the other was full of courage. But they were the same in this, that they loved Jesus; tried to follow His steps, honor His name, and spread His Gospel. From city to city, and from country to country, the glory of manhood and the beauty of youth went hand in hand: see how these Christians loved one another!

You know that St. Paul was at last put in prison at Rome. Even then, how much he wishes — more almost than at any other time, to have Timothy near him! He felt that his loving look and loving words would cheer, more than any other earthly thing, his gloomy dungeon. He says twice over, "Do thy diligence to come shortly" (2 Tim. 4:9). "Do thy diligence to come before winter" (2 Tim. 4:21). Just as we would say in writing to a friend, "Pray, do come, as fast as ever you can."

I often wonder if Timothy came in time to converse with his aged father before he died. I think St. Paul, even in writing that letter, was much afraid he would not see him again: and he therefore so words it, that it might be preserved as a keepsake by his dear son, and be read long after the writer of it had been laid in his grave. It reminds us of a bright ray bursting from the clouds in a dark and stormy sunset. No mother ever wrote a more beautiful letter to her absent boy than that second Epistle (to Timothy). How tender and faithful are the advices the Apostle gives! He seems afraid lest, when he himself has been martyred, Timothy may not be so stedfast as in former years. He pleads with him, among other things, to be true and constant. "But *continue* thou in the things which thou hast learnt" (2 Tim. 3:14). I should like to write that verse on every young heart. It is sad to think how many do not *"continue."* They sit like Timothy meekly at the feet of parents, and teachers, and ministers, when very young: but when they begin to grow bigger and get older, they often set aside the holy lessons of childhood and youth. They do not serve God or strive to please Him as once they did.

Beware of thus halting on the road; walking or running well for a time, but by and by beginning to loiter and linger, and then coming to a stop altogether. Remember, the mere fact of having pious fathers and mothers and friends, will not keep you from sin. Seek yourselves to set a strict and careful watch over your hearts. You cannot be too jealous about the inroads of temptation, or too much on your guard against the wiles of Satan. Note how St. Paul follows Timothy with earnest advices — "War a good warfare." "Hold fast." "Take heed." "Flee also youthful lusts." "Be strong." "Endure hardness." "Watch thou in all things." Oh, see that He who "walketh in the midst of the seven golden candlesticks," may not have too good reason to say that solemn word to some of you — "*Nevertheless,* I have somewhat against thee, because thou hast left thy first love!" Alas! alas! there have been many like Timothy who set out on the voyage of young life, with the white sails of faith and purity and earnestness bearing them on, — but they were induced to forget the helm of duty, and the compass of truth. They allowed themselves to drift among whirlpools and breakers, till they made shipwreck of faith and of a good conscience. They began, but they did not *"continue"* in the things which they had learned.

As a closing lesson from St. Paul's words, seek to value *"the Holy Scriptures."* They are "able," as in the case of Timothy, "to make you wise unto salvation" (2 Tim. 3:15). Timothy knew the Old Testament, and he was highly honored in having these two letters, or Epistles, of the New, specially addressed to him. You are far more favored than he. This Bible (including the Gospels and Epistles, a large part of which Timothy did not possess) is a golden 'Keepsake' sent to you from God. Prize it now, prize it to your last hour as your greatest blessing. Love God, as Timothy served Him. You can never expect to have so great and godly an Apostle and minister to be your companion and friend, and to write you letters, as he had. But you will have better. You will have *the Greatest* as your Friend. You will have *The King* — *"The King of Kings"* Himself giving you regal greetings, and saying, "Let the children of Zion be joyful in their King;" "I will be a Father unto you, and ye shall be My sons and daughters, saith the Lord Almighty."

In Rome, when visiting the vast, magnificent church, under the altar of which St. Paul himself is said to be buried and which is called by his name (San Paolo), it was to me a touching sight, that of a lowlier tomb immediately in front (the one close to the other), on which is inscribed in large lettering the simple name, *Timothei* (to Timothy). No one can rely on the truth of these traditions. In neither case may they be trusted. But it is surely interesting thus to see at the very same spot, the alleged resting-places of the two great Christian Apostles. Timothy was in Rome with his revered spiritual Father during the Apostle's first sojourn there (Phil. 1:1; Col. 1:1). So this at least we are sure of, that not far-off — in one of the houses of that ancient city, they must oft have met and conversed, sorrowed and rejoiced, wept and prayed together. Although I am not in the habit of placing any confidence, but the reverse, in the lying fables which abound about Apostles and Martyrs, I could not help wishing, in the present case at all events, that the tradition was a true one; — that this was, in a beautiful sense, a "family burying-ground" of the father and his "dear son in the faith"; that lovely and pleasant in their lives, in their death and in their graves they are not divided; — their bodies reposing side by side, in the sure and certain hope of a joyful resurrection.

At all events they have met now. "The good fight of faith" has been "fought" (1 Tim. 6:12), and in the presence of the Master they both so faithfully served, their spirits are rejoicing for ever and ever!

Standing in front of that double tomb with its circlet of burning lamps, one could repeat in silence over each, the appropriate lines of our own sweet poet; —

> "Soldier of Christ, well done!
> Rest from thy loved employ;
> The battle fought, the victory won,
> Enter thy Master's joy!
>
> The pains of death are past:
> Labor and sorrow cease:
> And life's long warfare closed at last,
> His soul is found in peace.

Soldier of Christ, well done!
Praise be thy new employ:
And, while eternal ages run,
Rest in thy Savior's joy!"

GOD, THE CHILDREN'S TEACHER (Ps. 71:17).

I. The Great Teacher.
  A. God is an effectual Teacher.
  B. God is a condescending Teacher.
  C. God is a loving Teacher.
  D. God is a wise Teacher.
  E. God is a needful Teacher.

II. The Lessons Which This Great Teacher Taught David.
  A. To value his soul.
  B. To value the world aright.
  C. To see his sin.
  D. Where the remedy was for all his sins.
  E. To live as in God's sight.
  F. He learnt to prepare to die.

III. When the Scholar Went to God's School.
  A. In his youth.
    1. Because it is such a happy school.
    2. Because they will not have so much to be sorry for afterwards.
    3. Because it will make them most useful.
    4. You will die soon.

IV. The Scholar — Where Is He? The Scholar — Where Is She?

A. I hope there are many who will be able to say, "O God, thou has taught me."   — C. H. SPURGEON.

(SERMON THEMES AND TEXTS)

1. A Command and a Promise, "Honor thy father and thy mother; that thy days may be long upon the land which the Lord thy God giveth thee" (Ex. 20:12).
2. Children a Blessing, "Lo, children are an heritage of the Lord" (Ps. 127:3).
3. Neglected Children, "A child left to himself bringeth his mother to shame" (Prov. 29:15).

4. Children Witnessing for Their Lord, "The children crying in the temple, and saying, Hosanna to the Son of David (Matt. 21:15).

FAR-SIGHTED

"Give me the children until they are seven and anyone may have them afterwards." — XAVIER.

NEVER TOO BUSY FOR A CHILD

St. Francis of Assisi was once very much occupied with some important work, and he gave orders to his attendants that he must on no account be disturbed. If anyone came desiring to see him, that one must be sent away. But after giving these strict orders, he paused and said, "But if a child should come —." That is what our Father in Heaven says. Perhaps, so busy in His universe is He, when men come as philosophers or theologians and knock at the door, they are not admitted, but if a child should come — which means, if any come in the child spirit of loving trust — the door is opened instantly. If a child should come — the Father is never too busy.

PRAYER FOR THE CHILDREN

Father, our children keep!
  We know not what is coming on the earth;
Beneath the shadow of Thy heavenly wing,
  O keep them, keep them, Thou who gav'st them birth.

Father, draw nearer us!
  Draw firmer round us Thy protecting arm;
Oh, clasp our children closer to Thy side,
  Uninjured in the day of earth's alarm.

Them in Thy chambers hide!
  Oh, hide them and preserve them calm and safe,
When sin abounds and error flows abroad,
  And Satan tempts, and human passions chafe.

Oh, keep them undefiled!
  Unspotted from a tempting world of sin;
That, clothed in white, through the bright city gates,
  They may with us in triumph enter in.
                              — HORATIUS BONAR.

IX. BACCALAUREATE

Religion and the Cultivation of the Intellect

LLEWELYN D. BEVAN

The Lord giveth wisdom — Proverbs 2:6

It is a serious evil if the best trained minds of the community are either hostile or indifferent to the claims of God. Students are placed in peculiar peril in respect of religion. There is a prevalent notion among half-educated people that the highest culture of the mind tends to the destruction of the religious spirit. There is now an antagonism between the school which prides itself upon its rationalism and the school which is equally entrenched in its strong faith. The habits of student life are not altogether helpful to the preservation of religious character. The studies, companions, work, and recreation, often operate injuriously upon the spiritual tone of men. Many, in the course of their study, have lost their faith.

I. *Religion in Relation to the Ends of Study*

There are specific subjects of study bearing direct relation to a man's life-work. But the real object of study is to discipline the powers and to strengthen the mind. Study which is intended to increase knowledge and to gather facts begins when student life ceases. The best student is the man who "is" most, not the man who has learned most. The highest ideal of study must be that which secures, or at least aims at securing, thoroughness of discipline and wholeness of view. Perfection, as the harmonious and free working of all parts and powers of the mind, must be the goal to which the student tends.

To learn everything is not given to man, but to be his best self in everything which he can be, this is his privilege. It is here that the subject of religion comes to be considered by the student. The nature which he possesses is distinctly religious. If a man does not attend to that faculty whereby he regards God, he neglects that part of himself which is most important and influential.

67

No man can afford to pass lightly by the claims upon him which are put forth by religion. The religious nature must be disciplined and cultured if we are to lay claim to wholeness of being.

See the influence which religion has exerted upon our human life and history. Eliminate religion from the story of the world and what is left? Critics charge religion with being a hindrance to human progress. But this is the common logical fallacy of putting the universal in place of the particular. Certain forms of religious polity may have done so, but not religion. Religion has, more than aught else, aided man in his long and weary pilgrimage of progress. Religion cannot be easily set aside by those who are engaged in the cultivation of the mind. All men are dealing with religious topics. The most striking instance is to be found in the modern teachers of science. Scarcely a single man of science of any repute but deals with these all-absorbing points of human thought, and indeed cannot help himself. Religion is human.

II. *Religion as an Influence of Deep and Far-reaching Power.*

The student cannot do his work as a common man. Intellectual cultivation is, as a rule, associated with moral refinement. The destruction of entire nature may be seen among students. This is generally preceded by neglect of the religious side of their nature — faith undermined either by the operations of intellectual doubt, or else still more seriously assailed by the numbing influences of sinful habits, but all proceeding in the first instance from the neglect of practical religion, the duties of prayer, and communion with God.

1. *Religion renders the student reverent.* Nothing is so unsuitable to the man who desires a cultivated mind as arrogance and self-esteem. All wisdom is humble. Reverence has been the mark of profound and patient investigators of nature in all ages. Religion and its duties produce reverence.

2. *Religion secures inward harmony of the powers.* Man cannot gain intellectual vigor when his whole being is torn asunder by conflicting forces. Outward physical quietness is the necessary condition of study. Inward spiritual peace is as necessary. Religion will give this. Coming into proper relation to God, we find everything else in its place. To return to God is to return to the balance of our life. The religious life is only sustained by the knowledge of Him who is the express image of the Father, and the shining ray of the central light of God. Christ's religion is the religion of intelligence.

Get busy (Mark 13:34)
    I.   FAITHFULLY
   II.   FRUITFULLY
  III.   EARNESTLY
   IV.   ABOUNDINGLY

— C. A. TERHUNE.

(SERMON THEMES AND TEXTS)
1. Building the House of Life, "Ye are God's building" (I Cor.
   3:9).
2. Hold Fast, "Take fast hold of instruction; let not her go;
   keep her; for she is thy life" (Prov. 4:13).
3. A Sound Foundation, "He is like a man that builded an house,
   and digged deep, and laid the foundation on a rock" (Luke
   6:48, 49).
4. Giving Heed to the Truth, "Therefore we ought to give more
   earnest heed to the things which we have heard, lest at any
   time we should let them slip" (Heb. 2:1).

MAKING A DREAM COME TRUE

A Scotch boy by the name of Alexander Duff had a dream in
which, in a chariot of great glory, God drew near to him where
he lay musing on a hillside, and calling to him said, "Come up,
hither; I have work for thee to do."

That vision never faded from his memory. He went to grammar school and to St. Andrews University, where a missionary
society was formed among the students, Duff becoming its first
librarian.

In 1829 he went out to India as the first missionary from the
Scottish church. He was a real pioneer. He opened a school in
Calcutta, and later helped to establish a medical college there.

If you have a dream of doing great service for God, try to
make it come true as Alexander Duff made his dream come true.

— SELECTED.

DEFINITIONS OF WISDOM

Wisdom consists chiefly in three things:
1. Knowledge to discern
2. Skill to judge
3. Activity to prosecute.

— T. WATSON.

WISDOM, HUMILITY OF

He who is convinced that he knows nothing of himself, as he ought to know, gives up steering his ship, and lets God put His hand on the rudder. He lays aside his own wisdom, and cries, "O God! my little wisdom is cast at Thy feet: my little judgment is given to Thee."

— SPURGEON.

Make my mortal dreams come true,
    with the work I fain would do;
Clothe with life the weak intent,
    let me be the thing I meant;
Let me find in Thy employ,
    peace that dearer is than joy.

— JOHN GREENLEAF WHITTIER.

Greatly begin! though thou have time
But for a line, be that sublime —
Not failure, but low aim is crime.

— JAMES RUSSELL LOWELL.

O, to be something, something!
    Where others Thy likeness may see;
That self may be lost in service,
    And our lives glorify Thee.
Ready to work or to suffer,
    Whichever Thy love shall command;
Secure — whether shadow or sunshine,
    They are all from Thy loving hand.

—IDA TREMAIN.

X. INDEPENDENCE DAY

Freedom and Law

HENRY P. LIDDON

I Peter 2:16

Freedom is one of those words which need no recommendation: it belongs to the same category as light, order, progress, law. It is one of the ideas which, in some sense or other, mankind accepts as an axiom; as a landmark or principle of healthful life which is beyond discussion. What do we mean by freedom? We mean the power of a living being to act without hindrance to the true law of its life.

I. Christ has given men *political or social freedom*.

He has not indeed drawn out a scheme of government, and stamped it with His divine authority as guaranteeing freedom. Yet with our Lord there came the germs of political liberty. When individual man had learnt to feel the greatness and the interest of life; the real horizon which stretches out before the soul's eye beyond the grave; the depths of being within the soul; its unexhausted capacities for happiness and for suffering; the reality and nearness of God, of His Divine Son, of our fellow-citizens the blessed angels; the awful, inexpressible distinction of being redeemed from death by the blood of the Most Holy, and sanctified by the Eternal Spirit; it was impossible not to feel also that each man had, in the highest sense, rights to assert and a bearing to maintain. Thus a Christian was a free man, simply because he was a Christian.

It has often been alleged that, as a matter of fact, our Lord left the great despotisms of the world for a while untouched. Jesus Christ taught, He was crucified, He rose, He ascended. But the Caesar Tiberius still sat upon the throne of the Roman world. There never was a more odious system of personal government than that of the Roman Emperors; the surviving forms of the extinct republic did but make the actual tyranny which

71

had succeeded it more hard to bear. Yet it was of such an Emperor as Nero that St. Paul wrote (Rom. 13:1); and St. Peter (chap. 2:13, 14). And in the same way apostles advise Christian slaves to give obedience to their masters as unto the Lord; to obey, not with eye-service, as if they had only to do as much as might be insisted on by a jealous owner, but with singleness of heart, as men who throw every energy into their work. It may be asked, How are such precepts compatible with the assertion that Christ gave us political freedom? The answer is that He gave us a moral force which did two things. First, it made every Christian independent of outward political circumstances; and, secondly, it made the creation of new civil institutions only a question of time.

II.   Christ gave men also *intellectual freedom.*

He enfranchised them by the gift of truth. He gave truth in its fulness; truth not merely relative and provisional, but absolute and final. Until He came the human intellect was enslaved. It was enslaved either to degrading superstition, or to false and one-sided philosophies. When Christ, in all the glory of His Godhead and His Manhood, had enthroned Himself in the soul, He taught men to think worthily of the greatness of God and of the greatness of man, notwithstanding man's weakness and corruption. He freed men from all the cramping influences of local philosophies, of local teachers, of petty schemes and theories for classes and races. He led men out into the great highways of thought, where, if they would, they might know the universal Father, manifested in His Blessed Son, as the Author of all existence, as its object, and as its end. Certainly our Lord has given us a body of Truth, which we can, if we like, reject, but which it is our happiness to believe. What He did for men in this way is embodied in His own teaching, in the writings of His apostles, and in the creeds of the universal Church. These are to intellectual liberty what law is to social liberty. They protect, they do not cramp it. They furnish a fixed point, from which thought may take wing.

III.   Christ has made men *morally free.*

He has broken the chains which fettered the human will, and has restored to it its buoyancy and its power. What had been lost was more than regained in Christ. Not merely was the penalty of old transgressions paid, so that man was redeemed from a real captivity: but the will was reinvigorated by a Heaven-sent force or grace, once more placing it in true harmony with the law of man's life (Rom. 6:18). Here it is objected that moral freedom is not worth having if it be only a service after all. "You talk of freedom," men say, "but you mean rule. You mean restrictions upon action; restrictions upon inclination; restrictions upon speech. You mean obligations: obligations to work; obligations to self-discipline; obligations to sacrifice self to others; obligations to all the details of Christian duty." You are right: certainly we do. A Christian lives under a system of restrictions and obligations; and yet he is free. Those obligations and restrictions only prescribe for him what his own new heaven-sent nature would wish to be and to do. Whatever a Christian may be outwardly, he is inwardly a free man. In obeying Christ's law he acts as he desires to act: he acts according to this, the highest law of his life, because he rejoices to do so. He obeys law; the Law of God. But then he has no inclination to disobey it. He is, as St. Peter says, a servant of God; but then, as he would not for all the world be anything else, his service is perfect freedom.

(SERMON THEMES AND TEXTS)

1. The Basis for National Blessedness, "Blessed is the Nation whose God is the Lord" (Ps. 33:12).
2. The Source of National Greatness, "Righteousness exalteth a nation: but sin is a reproach to any people" (Prov. 14:34).
3. The Proper Attitude towards Governmental Authority, "Let every soul be subject unto the higher power. For there is no power but of God" (Rom. 13:15).
4. The Causes of War, "From whence come wars and fightings among you?" (James 4:1).

LIBERTY AND LAW

"Ye shall know the truth, and the truth shall make you free." There is, then, no liberty for humanity, but the liberty which flames out from God's law of truth. The most independent and happy moment of life is when a soul can say: "I'm a slave of Jesus." It is the soul's true declaration of independence.

— SELECTED.

TRUE THEN — TRUE NOW

"Our civilization cannot survive materially unless it be redeemed spiritually. It can be saved only by becoming permeated with the spirit of Christ and being made free and happy by the practices which spring out of the spirit. Only thus can discontent be driven out and all the shadows lifted from the road ahead."

         — WOODROW WILSON.

> 'Tis liberty alone that gives the flow'r
> Of fleeting life its lustre and perfume,
> And we are weeds without it.
>
>   — COWPER.

> License they mean when they cry Liberty!
> For who loves that must first be wise and good.
>
>   — JOHN MILTON.

LORD, WHILE FOR ALL MANKIND WE PRAY

> Lord, while for all mankind we pray,
> Of every clime and coast,
> O hear us for our native land,
> The land we love the most.
>
> O guard our shores from every foe:
> With peace our borders bless;
> With prosperous times our cities crown,
> Our fields with plenteousness.
>
> Unite us in the sacred love
> Of knowledge, truth, and Thee;
> And let our hills and valleys shout
> The songs of liberty.
>
> Lord of the nations, to Thee
> Our country we commend;
> Be Thou her refuge and her trust,
> Her everlasting friend.
>
>   — JOHN WREFORD.

XI. LABOR DAY

Christian Servants

By J. Cohen

Servants, be obedient to them that are your masters according to the flesh, with fear and trembling, in singleness of your heart, as unto Christ. — Eph. 6:5.

The Christian servants at Ephesus, who first read this letter of the apostle, were, probably, many of them slaves. Some, no doubt, were hired servants; but perhaps the greater part were in a state of absolute bondage to heathen masters.

I. Let us look, first, *at the precepts and directions given to servants.*

And one is struck with this: there is no hint thrown out, no suggestion whatever offered, as to its being right or necessary to quit one's occupation in order to serve Christ and promote His cause in the world. It is not an infrequent thought, in the minds especially of young men, when brought to the Lord, that they must give up their worldly occupation, and devote themselves wholly and exclusively to minister in holy things. And now let us notice the particulars which the apostle expressly mentions for a Christian servant to attend to.

1. Observe the first command is *obedience*: "Servants, be obedient to your masters according to the flesh."

2. Further, in this preceptive part of his address, notice, secondly, how he enjoins a thorough *devotedness* to his master's interests. This will appear in making manifest your thorough trustworthiness and faithfulness. I do not speak of mere honesty; the apostle means much more than this, when he speaks of "showing all good fidelity." There is such a thing as seeking just to go through the daily routine with the spirit of a hireling, who will do no more than he must; who needs to be well looked after, or he will leave much neglected. Quite different is the spirit of a Christian servant; he will try his very utmost to please his em-

ployer; but he has a higher aim. What a pattern of this was Abraham's servant Eleazar, and Jacob in Laban's house, and Joseph in his captivity: first, in Potiphar's house, and then in his dungeon: his master "left all he had in Joseph's hand; he knew not ought he had, save the bread he did eat." No terms could more emphatically give the idea of perfect freedom from all care, produced and maintained by the perfect assurance of ability, assiduity, and incorruptible rectitude.

II. But let us proceed to notice, secondly, *the motive which the apostle holds up as the governing principle, the ruling motive of a truly Christian servant.*

"As the servants of Christ, doing the will of God from the heart." "Whatsoever ye do, do it heartily: as to the Lord, and not unto men"; "for ye serve the Lord Christ." Again: "That ye may adorn" — ye servants, plain, humble, unnoticed, who have little to set you off in the eyes of the world — "that ye may adorn the doctrine of God our Savior in all things." In a word, let there be at the root of all — godliness: "Setting the Lord always before you."

1. Now, first, what a *comprehensive principle* is this! It reminds us of those wonderful triumphs of mechanical skill by which the same engine can be applied to lift the most ponderous masses, or to drive with the utmost delicacy, as with the feeble blow of an infant, the slenderest pin into its place. So with this principle of doing all as to the Lord.

2. And then, secondly, how *ennobling and elevating a motive* it is! The highest archangel knows no higher.

3. And then, thirdly, how *consoling and comforting a motive* is this to the humble Christian! "I am poor and needy, but the Lord careth for me," may he say. "One need not be in high station to serve the Savior."

III. And then, thirdly, *let us not forget the promise annexed to it.*

"Knowing, that whatsoever good thing any man doeth, the same shall he receive of the Lord, whether he be bond or free." Oh! how often this is manifested even here in this life! Many are the houses where the pious servant has been the first to introduce the gospel, and by his "patient continuance in well-doing," has demonstrated its reality and power.

OCCUPY TILL I COME

And he called his ten servants, and delivered them
ten pounds, and said unto them, Occupy till I come.
—Luke 6:13.

We have four things here, which keeping to the metaphor of
the text, I may designate as the *Capital,* the *Business,* the *Profits,*
and the *Audit.*

I. *The Capital.* A pound was a very little thing for a prince
who was going to get a kingdom to leave with his servants to
trade upon. The smallness of the gift is, I think, an essential
part of the representation. May it not be intended to point out
to us this lesson — how small after all, even the high gift that we
all receive alike here is, in comparison with what we are des-
tined to receive when the kingdom comes? Even the salvation
that is in Jesus Christ, as it is at present experienced on earth,
is but like the one poor pound that was given to the servants, as
compared with the unspeakable wealth that shall be theirs —
the ten cities, the five cities, and all the glories of supremacy and
sovereignty, when He comes.

II. *The Trading.* You Christian men and women ought to
make your Christian life and your Christian service a matter
of business. Put the same virtues into it that some of you put
into your trade. Your best business in this world, as the Shorter
Catechism has it, is to glorify God and to enjoy Him for ever.
And the salvation that you have, you have to trade upon, to make
a business of, to work it out, in order that, by working it out,
by living upon it, and living by it, applying its principles to
daily life, and seeking to spread it among other people, it may
increase and fructify in your hands.

III. *The Profits.* The immediate results are in direct corre-
spondence and proportion to the immediate activity and diligence.
The truths that you live by, you will believe more because you
live by them. The faculties that you employ in Christ's service
will grow and increase by reason of your employment of them.

IV. *The Audit.* "Till I come," or, "Whilst I am coming."
As if all through the ages the king was coming, coming nearer.
We have to work as remembering that everyone of us shall give
an account of himself and his trading unto the Proprietor when
He comes back.

THE JUBILEE; OR, THE DEGENERATIVE AND CORRECTIVE FORCES OF SOCIETY

I. The Degenerative Forces of Society are in Itself Debt, Slavery, Poverty, Materialism.

II. The Corrective Forces of Society are from God.

1. Man is superior to property.

The violation of this truth is the ruin of society, and it is violated every day.

2. God is the disposer of property.

"The earth is the Lord's and the fulness thereof."

3. Society has higher wants than property. Spiritual services.
— THE HOMILIST.

(SERMON THEMES AND TEXTS)

1. The Dignity of Service, "I am among you as he that serveth" (Luke 22:27).
2. The Unbrotherly Question, "Am I my brother's keeper?" (Gen. 4:9).
3. Work Heartily Done, "Whatsoever thy hand findeth to do, do it with thy might" (Eccl. 9:10).
4. The Labor Principle, "To each one his work" (Mark 13:34).

SOLUTION OF INDUSTRIAL PROBLEMS.

This hope is bright in exact proportion as the Gospel of Christ is applied to the burning industrial questions.

VALUE OF LABOR

God is constantly teaching us that nothing valuable is ever obtained without labor; and that no labor can be honestly expended without our getting its value in return. He is not careful to make everything easy to man. The Bible itself is no light book; human duty no holiday engagement. The grammar of deep personal religion, and the grammar of real practical virtue, are not to be learned by any easy methods. — BINNEY.

CHARACTER OF LABOR.

Labor is life: from the inmost heart of the worker rises his God-given Force—the sacred celestial life-essence breathed into him by the Almighty God! — CARLYLE.

THE NIGHT COMETH

Work, for the night is coming;
  Work, through the morning hours;
Work, while the dew is sparkling;
  Work, 'mid springing flowers;
Work, when the day grows brighter,
  Work, in the glowing sun;
Work, for the night is coming,
  When man's work is done.

Work, for the night is coming,
  Work through the sunny noon;
Fill brightest hours with labor,
  Rest comes sure and soon.
Give every flying minute
  Something to keep in store:
Work, for the night is coming,
  When man works no more.

Work, for the night is coming,
  Under the sunset skies;
While their bright tints are glowing,
  Work, for the daylight flies.
Work till the last beam fadeth,
  Fadeth to shine no more;
Work while the night is darkening,
  When man's work is o'er.

— S. DYER.

Labor is good for a man, bracing up his energies to conquest,
And without it life is dull, the man perceiving himself useless:
For wearily the body groaneth, like a door on rusty hinges.

— TUPPER.

Free man freely work:
Whoever fears God, fears to sit at ease.

— E. B. BROWNING.

appoint a day of thanksgiving. This was accordingly done, and the custom has been continued ever since.

— MORIER.

THANKSGIVING DAY

Great as the preparations were for the dinner, everything was so contrived that not a soul in the house should be kept from the morning service of Thanksgiving in the church.

— H. B. STOWE.

THANKSGIVING — in the Heart

As flowers carry dewdrops, trembling on the edges of the petals, and ready to fall at the first waft of wind or brush of bird, so the heart should carry its beaded words of thanksgiving; and at the first breath of heavenly flavour, let down the shower, perfumed with the heart's gratitude.

— H. W. BEECHER.

Thanksgiving day, I fear,
If one the solemn truth must touch,
Is celebrated, not so much
To thank the Lord for blessings o'er,
As for the sake of getting more!

— WILL CARLETON.

THANKSGIVING

Our heartfelt thanks we offer Thee,
    Our Father, God,
For all the blessings full and free,
    By Thee bestowed.

For the year's great prosperity,
    Our praise ascends,
And sweeter comforts lent by Thee —
    A home and friends.

The full and plenteous harvest store,
    And fruitage fair.
All with unnumbered tokens more,
    Thy love declare.

For blessings of each passing hour —
    Things fair to see —
The sunshine and refreshing shower,
    As sent by Thee.

For all of nature's beauties bright,
    In grand array —
All the fair glory of the night,
    And fairer day.

And Thou wilt be our sure defense,
    When death draws near —
E'en pain assumes a sweeter sense,
    If Thy grace cheer.

And so our thanks to Thee we bring,
    And filial love —
And join with heart and voice, to sing
    With saints above.

                        — MRS. M. E. LEONHARDT.

XIII. CHRISTMAS

We Three Kings of Orient Are

DAVID JAMES BURRELL

Seek and ye shall find. — MATT. 7:7.

Run ye to and fro, and see now if there be any that seeketh the truth. — JER. 5:1.

For this is good and acceptable in the sight of God our Savior, who will have all men to come unto the knowledge of the truth. — I TIM. 2:3, 4.

Jesus saith, I am the truth. — JOHN 14:6.

Now when Jesus was born in Bethlehem of Judea in the days of Herod the king, behold there came wise men from the east to Jerusalem, saying, Where is he that is born king of the Jews? for we have seen his star in the east and are come to worship him. — MATT. 2:1, 2.

The king of Judea was troubled. It was rumored that about this time, in fulfilment of prophecy, a Prince was to be born, who would assume the Jewish throne. Tacitus declares that the opinion was prevalent in the East that the Messiah of Israel was about to appear. Vergil had written his fourth Eclog, in which he announced the near approach of the golden age. A feeling of expectancy was prevalent everywhere. Herod was an old man, but still tenacious of his ill-gotten power. He was an apostate Jew, who long ago had forsaken the religion of his fathers to enter the service of the Roman government. His career had been a brilliant one; a *protege* of Antony, he had at a very early age, been made governor of Galilee and afterward tetrarch of Judea. He was a man of vast ambition; shrewd, cunning, and of violent passions; not above the trick of a demagog, he has nevertheless possessed of much cleverness and a vast executive ability. To please his royal master, he built the splendid city of Caesarea. To conciliate the Jews, whom he hated he rebuilt their temple and splendidly adorned it.

In the porch of this temple the old king was walking nearly nineteen hundred years ago. His purple robes sparkled with gems and precious stones; a glorious ruby blazed in his turban; but his restless eyes betrayed a troubled heart. Off yonder, beyond the Kedron, a group of venerable strangers drew near, their long garments covered with dust. They would have attracted attention anywhere. Entering at the eastern or Shushan gate, they climbed the marble stairway of the temple, entered Solomon's porch, and would have passed on into the inner courts but for the admonition of a Levite, who pointed to an inscription on the middle wall of partition, "Let no Gentile or unclean person enter here under the penalty of death." Arrested by this rebuff, they said, "We have come from the far East, seeking Him who is born King of the Jews. Tell us where we may find Him." A moment later they were engaged in conversation with Herod. "Whence come ye?" "From the East." "And your errand?" "To find the promised King of the Jews." "It's a fool's errand; I alone am king of the Jews." "Nay, we cannot be mistaken, for we have come under Divine guidance."

And thereupon they told their story — how as they were watching the stars according to their custom, and meditating on the great promise of the coming Deliverer, a new luminary wheeled into view and seemed to beckon to them. Was this a harbinger of that event for which they looked? While they wondered, it moved on toward the West and they arose and followed it. Their hope had been that the Jewish Prince would be found in the Holy City, and they were amazed to find that nothing was here known of Him. The wise men were detained while at Herod's order the members of the Sanhedrin came together to consult as to the rumored birth of this Prince. They agreed as to the prophecy; the event was to occur in Bethlehem: "And thou Bethlehem, in the land of Judah, are not the least among the princes of Judah, for out of thee shall come a governor that shall rule my people Israel." The wise men were then permitted to resume their journey, with a parting injunction that they should return and report as to the success of their singular quest. As they resumed their journey, lo, yonder in the heavens a star moved along before them, and they followed with great joy.

We may find profit in the contemplation of the deed of these pilgrims on this Christmas Sunday. From time immemorial they have been regarded as kings:

"We three kings of orient are,
Bearing gifts, we journey afar;
O'er field and fountain, moor and mountain,
Following yonder star."

In the cathedral at Cologne there is a golden reliquary in which are preserved, in the odor of sanctity, the relics of these men. I said to the venerable monk in attendance, "Do you really believe that these are the relics of the wise men?" "Oh, yes," he replied. "There is no question whatever as to their genuineness; we know their names — Gaspar, Melchior, and Balthazar. The venerable Bede tells all about them." There is, however, considerable doubt — to put it mildly — as to the trustworthiness of the legends which have gathered about these Magi. We have no reason to suppose they were kings, but we know they were truth-seekers; and, as Cromwell said to his daughter, "To be a truth-seeker is to be the best sect next to a truth-finder."

I. *The Quest.* Wisdom is the principal thing, and there is nothing better than to get understanding. All truth is worth having. We blame our children for being inquisitive. But why? John Locke said, "The way to get knowledge is to ask questions." A wiser still has said, "Seek, and ye shall find." The cure for doubt is not a hoodwink, but a telescope. All truth is worth the having, and therefore, worth the seeking. "Eureka!" cried Archimedes over a certain mathematical discovery. In all the world there is no pursuit so ennobling, so inspiring, and so gladdening as the pursuit of truth. This holds in all the provinces, but especially in the province of spiritual things.

A man is in his noblest attitude when confronting the great spiritual verities. In this we are distinguished from the lower orders of life. We are able to touch the tremendous problems and measurably to solve them; and herein is the sweetest of life's delights. Lord Bacon said: "It is a pleasure to stand upon the shore and see ships tossing far away upon the sea; it is a pleasure to stand in the castle window and look down upon the battle and the adventures thereof; but no pleasure is comparable to the standing upon the vantage-ground of truth and beholding spiritual things."

II. *The Harbinger.* God helps every man who earnestly desires to solve the problem of destiny. To these wise men He gave the guiding star. A vast amount of erudition has been spent in the attempt to get rid of the supernatural on these premises. It is said that a remarkable conjunction of certain planets occurred at about this time. In 1604 Kepler saw in the heavens a phenomenon which occurs only once in nearly a thousand years : Saturn and Jupiter were in conjunction; presently Mars also wheeled into line, thus forming "A fiery Trygon in Pisces." The constellation of Pisces, or the fish was regarded as symbolical of Judea. The fish was also used by the early Christians as an anagram of Christ. Thus the "fiery Trygon" was identified with the star of Bethlehem. It is a fascinating hypothesis, but unfortunately (1) it did not occur at the precise time of the advent; and (2) being at an altitude of fifty-seven degrees, it could not have paused over a village or a particular home. We are, therefore, led to regard the star as a special messenger — an angel with a torch, as it were — sent to direct these wise men in their earnest quest. So God interposes in behalf of every sincere seeker for truth. "Seek, and ye shall find."

It was many years ago that a butcher's boy went singing ribald songs about the streets of Nottingham. A taste for knowledge brought him to Cambridge University, where he distinguished himself not only for his cleverness as a student but as a reviler of Christ. By the unexpected death of a companion he was brought to think seriously of eternal things; his sins weighed heavily upon him; but at Calvary he found pardon. In the early flush of his conversion he wrote his gratitude in the familiar hymn:

> "Once on the raging seas I rode;
>   The storm was loud, the night was dark,
> The ocean yawned, and rudely blowed
>   The wind that tossed my foundering bark.
> Deep horror then my vitals froze;
>   Death-stuck, I ceased the tide to stem,
> When suddenly a star arose:
>   It was the Star of Bethlehem!
>
> "It was my guide, my light, my all;
>   It bade my dark forebodings cease,
> And through the storm and danger's thrall
>   It led me to the port of peace.
> Now safely moored, my perils o'er,
>   I'll sing, first in night's diadem,
> For ever and forevermore,
>   The Star, the Star of Bethlehem!"

God never yet left a man in the lurch who sincerely desired to solve the problem of destiny. It is a true saying, "A seeking sinner finds a seeking Savior."

III. *The Treasure-Trove*. The wise men have reached their destination. All the divinely kindled stars lead to Bethlehem. Here is the end of the great quest. The star that guided the Magi rested over a humble cottage. They entered and found the Christ-child — a child upon its mother's breast! Is that all? Ay, all — everything! In this child all the streams of prophecy converge. From this child radiate all the glowing lines of history. In this humble home at Bethlehem all the hopes of Abraham, the dreams of David, and the visions of Isaiah are realized. This cottage is the center of the world.

Are you, friend, seeking the truth? Follow your star. Hearken when God speaks. "There are so many voices, and none of them is without significance." It is easy to quench all lights; to hush all voices; but hearken and give heed. Bethlehem is not far ahead. "Press on!" as Cromwell, the Lord Protector, said to his daughter, "press on, dear heart, and thou shalt find the satisfying portion. Let nothing cool thy ardor until thou find it."

So here are the Magi opening their packs before the Christ-child. The search is over; the problem of destiny is solved. Here is gold for the King; here is myrrh for the Victor; here is frankincense for very God of very God. We are celebrating now the infinite grace that lavished upon us the unspeakable gift, and what shall we render in return? I beseech you brethren, by His great mercy, that ye present yourselves, a living sacrifice; which is your reasonable service.

(Adapted)

JOY AT THE BIRTH OF JESUS (Luke 2:10)

To us men, more than to the angels or to any other created beings, is this day's joy. It is the great festival of humanity. He who was born today was —

I. *A Redeemer*

Delivering us from the servitude of sin and Satan — a worse bondage than that of Egypt. Think what songs of praise (Ex. 15:1) are due to Jesus Christ today, who, by the baptism reddened by His blood, hath delivered us from the power our spiritual foes.

II. *A Surety*
Taking upon Himself all our debts and the condemnation of
their punishment. A new, the greatest and unheard-of benefit
(Col. 2:14). He came today to remit that vast debt of sin which
God alone could pay; that the bond might be burnt in the fire
of His love, or be affixed to the cross on Mount Calvary.

III. *A Heavenly Physician*
Prepared and willing to heal all diseases, again and again,
without fee or reward, without pain to the patient (Matt. 9:12;
Luke 4:23).

IV. *A Sun to the World*
Enlightening a darkness more dense than any natural or physical darkness (John 1:9; 9:5). A light —
    1. Eternal
    2. Cheering
    3. Glorifying

V. *A Guide to the True and Blessed Life* (Micah 2:13) Going
before in difficulties, smoothing rough ways.

VI. *A Nourisher of the World*
Sustaining us in the way with "living bread."

VII. *A Prince of Peace*
Bringing peace —
    1. With God
    2. To one's own conscience
    3. With each other. (Ps. 11:6-10)

VIII. *A Savior*
Who will, after this life bring us safely to the blessed and
eternal country and being. Think on all these things and say
(Ps. 117:1).   — M. FABER.

(SERMON THEMES AND TEXTS)

1. A Visit to Bethlehem, "Let us now go even to Bethlehem, and
   see this thing which is come to pass, which the Lord hath
   made known to us" (Luke 2:15).
2. The Miraculous Birth, "That holy thing which shall be born
   of thee shall be called the Son of God" (Luke 1:35).
3. Thanksgiving at Christmastide, "Thanks be to God for his
   unspeakable gift" (II Cor. 9:15).
4. A Proper Question on Christmas Day, "What think ye of
   Christ" (Matt. 22:42).

BIRTH OF CHRIST

The death of Christ is a great mystery; but his birth is even a greater. That he should live a human life at all, is stranger than that, so living, he should die a human death. I can scarce get past his cradle in my wondering, to wonder at his cross. The infant Jesus is, in some views, a greater marvel than Jesus with the purple robe and the crown of thorns. — CRICHTON.

INCARNATION OF CHRIST

That He should be the seed of the woman was made known to Adam, but not of what nation till Abraham, nor of what tribe till Jacob, nor of what sex till David, nor whether born of a virgin till Isaiah. Thus by degrees was that great mystery of godliness revealed to mankind. If any Jew object, saith Chrysostom, How could a virgin bring forth? — Ask him, How could Sarah, when old and barren, bear a child? The bees have young, yet know not marriage. This Head-stone of the corner was cut out of the mountain without hands; this flower of the field, this rose of Sharon, hath heaven for His father, and earth for His mother. Was it not as easy to frame this second Adam in the womb, as that first Adam out of the mire?

— J. TRAPP.

Christians awake, salute the happy morn,
Whereon the Saviour of the world was born.
— JOHN BYROM.

I heard the bells on Christmas Day
Their old familiar carols play,
    And wild and sweet
    The words repeat
Of peace on earth, good-will to men!
— LONGFELLOW.

God rest ye, little children; let nothing you affright,
For Jesus Christ, your Saviour, was born this happy night;
Along the hills of Galilee the white flocks sleeping lay,
When Christ, the Child of Nazareth, was born on Christmas
    day.
— D. M. MULOCK.

This happy day, whose risen sun
Shall set not through eternity,
This holy day when Christ the Lord,
Took on Him our humanity.
     — Phoebe Cary.

Light of the world so clear and bright,
Enter our homes this Christmas night;
Re-light our souls so tenderly,
That we may grow to be like Thee.
     — Anonymous.

XIV. OLD YEAR'S DAY

The Right Way

J. VAUGHAN

And he led them forth by the right way, that they might go to a city of habitation. — Psalm 107:7.

We cannot really judge of things until we have seen the whole of them. And, as no one has seen the whole of his own like, no one can form a true judgment of his life. And even if a man could see the whole of his own life, still, as he cannot know all its bearings upon other lives, he would be an imperfect judge. And no life — nor any event in any life — is an isolated thing; so that we are driven to the conclusion that the only mind which could take it in, which could take in the whole life of one man, and all the lives of all men, is Omniscience. Only Omniscience can really judge anything!

But, as time goes on, we all learn to qualify our judgments, and rectify many mistakes which we made about our own lives. For, what was once a subject of pure faith, becomes a matter of actual experience. Promises grow into facts. Many things we thought wrong turn out to have been quite right. Things which seemed to be 'all against us,' Jacob-like, we find to have been quite *for us.* Our worst trials our best blessings!

For, as life goes on, we see ends. And we can more humbly wait and expect what it will be when the end of ends comes. Already, our God has justified Himself.

And, if it were only for this, we ought to be better, as we get older, for we are able to see what once was only a matter of trust. Evil turns out very good. The mysteries of one period are the very lights which shine most brightly in another. God we find so very wise, and we were very foolish; and we can put-to our seal, and say, of many a thing of which we once complained and condemned, "It was a right way."

And now we have come to another of those high ridges on the road, on which it is well that the traveller stop a moment, and take his reckoning of the journey. Such as perhaps Moses took when, from the top of Nebo, he might be able at once to see both the land of promise, as it lay at his feet, and the tract which he had gone in the desert, stretching out behind him.

And we, looking back this day on the way we have come, are helped, by the experience of another year, to take a truer retrospect. And, though many spots in it may be still wrapped in clouds, and we cannot explain them, yet other things, once as dark, have come out so clear that even reason and knowledge can help faith the more to write upon it all, "The right way!" "The right way!"

And remember, when I say "The right way," it means not "the right way" generally and abstractedly, but "the right way" *for me.* The "way" I could bear; the "way" I wanted; the best for my character and my strength: "the right way" for me.

Now, concerning that "right way," I wish you first to notice that the record does not run, *"They went* the right way," but *"He led them* by the right way." And who ever found "the right way" who was not *"led"?* And if you have gone any very really *wrong way* this year, was not it only because you either did not look out for *the leadings,* or you did not follow them when you saw them?

Have not all the great mistakes of your life been that you went *before* God? You did not ask for tokens; or you did not wait for tokens; or you did not believe in tokens; or you did not obey tokens! You neglected the signals! What wonder if there were disasters, if not wrecks!

But if *He* "leads," not only is the path safe, but *He* is there; and the straighter you walk, the nearer you are to Him; and that makes more than safety, — presence, life, communion, joy!

But there is a part of God's leadings which we must not overlook — *hedgings.* Israel was stopped and hedged in many times in the wilderness. They must not start, when they wanted to start: they must not go back, when they wanted to go back. They were prevented from going to this great country, and to that country.

You would miss a great deal of *the leadings* if you fail to notice and respect the hedgings. I should not say the hedgings are better than the leadings. But the hedgings are often very sharp!

Let us look at one or two of the particular features of the leadings in the wilderness. It may be we shall find the counter-

part in some things which have happened to us during the past
year.

The Israelites had a very little way to go, and they were a
very long time about it. What seemed a matter of days, took
many years. When they first set out, they must have thought that
they would have reached the end in a very short space. But it
proved a weary length, and they were kept the longest in very
unlikely places. Especially just as they were on the very borders
of their home.

This must have looked to them anything but "right." But it
was "right." There were reasons that they never guessed, the
other side of Jordan, in the land of Canaan; and they themselves
— though they knew it not — were not ripe, they were not ready
for the rest.

Is it so with you? Have you been a very long time getting on
a very little way? At the first, but especially at the last, did
heaven seem to you to get further and further off, and did you
doubt, and question, and wonder why what was expected to be
so quick, was so exceedingly slow? And have you lived all this
time and found no reason?

The fightings of God's people in the wilderness were all at the
beginning and at the end of it. It is generally so with God's
saints. There are some very hard battles as they set out upon
their new way, to heaven — for God always tries and exercises
the grace that He has given. But the hardest, if I mistake not,
will be at the last, even at the threshold.

Have you found anything like this?

And they had strange ups and downs. Their road, as we trace
it on the map, is a perfect riddle. Now quite near, and then back
again, far, far away, almost to where they set out.

Perhaps some of us can tell to-day a like story!

And it was all in dependence — most absolute and humble dependence for everything. They could look to themselves for
nothing. Not a drop nor a crumb, nothing came from the wilderness, — all direct from God Himself.

It was all trust. They had to trust for the morrow. But it all
came, — sure, regular, abundant.

And who ever went the road to heaven without learning — tem-
porally and spiritually — the same humiliating but assuring lesson?

And the leading was the clearest where the need was the greatest. The cloud by day, the light by night. God's universal method.

In our sunny days, His hand dimly seen, and His voice low. But in our darkest hours, bright, distinct, glorious!

Still, it was a restless life they lived these forty years. In tents, which they pitched, and had soon to strike. Always shifting, always moving. And they scarcely knew when or where.

Just as perhaps life has lately been to some of us. The old things seem strangely to be breaking up, and very unsettled. Nothing continuing in one stay. So that sometimes life has seemed a mere *mirage,* made up of dissolving views, one after another, melting away at the touch!

And why this to them? And why to us? The answer is simple. *It is not home.* We are but "strangers and pilgrims." We must sit loose, and not tarry long by the way. It is "the right way," *but it is only "a way."* And we are prone to say, "It was good for me to be here!" and mistake our "tabernacles" for our "houses," while He is all the while leading us forth to "go to a city of habitation."

The expression, "city of habitation," of course, is intended to contrast with the tent of the wilderness. And our Saviour (in His and His disciples' bitter hour of separation) had the same thought probably in His mind when, sad at the going out and coming in which make our world, He said, "In My Father's house are many *mansions,"* abiding-places; resting-places. Not like this! Where there shall be no parting, but, as St. John saw it, "they shall be as pillars in the temple of our God," on which the very stability of the whole building depends: "they shall be as pillars in the temple of our God, and shall go no more out."

That will be the place, that will be the time to see how "right the way" was, when looking back, "a thousand years will look as one day, and one day as a thousand years," for we shall look with the eye of God; and we shall see and know how "the humblings" and "the provings" were all "to do us good in our latter end"; and how we were being educated up, I do not say to the dignities, and the duties, and the privileges of the citizenship of that 'city of habitation;' but each one of us to our own particular spot and sphere, which we are to occupy in that glorious "city."

Not one sorrow, not trouble, not one tear, not one mortification, not one fall too many. They were "the *right* way"; they were the *only* way"; they were *His* "way" to heaven.

But, oh! the contrast of this life of folly to that world of reality!

Here, the strongest of our poor little structures falls, because it has no corner-stone. But *there* is "the city that hath *foundations, whose* Builder and Maker is God!"

Here, families outgrow their houses, and people find their native land too small, and men are forced to go out and colonize, to fulfill the first primary law given to man, to "replenish the whole earth." But *there,* are habitations large enough for all, and dwelling-places where families will never separate!

Here, the weary pilgrims toil their desert way. But *there,* the traveller has laid down his staff for the sweet eternity of rest.

Here, the years roll round and round their course. The old year wanes, and leaves its chasms, and its reproachful memories! — the thousand things left undone, and all that is done, done so badly; and the New Year comes in, and brings its uncertainties and its fears. But *there,* where nothing clashes, there shall be room for every duty, and space for every affection, in the unsinning and unanxious solaces of the perpetual freshness of one eternity of love.

And when there we read the little chapter of life, this will be the sum and substance of the history: — "He led them forth by the right way, that they might go to a city of habitation!"

REDEEMING THE TIME (Eph. 5:16)

I. SOME REASONS FOR REDEEMING THE TIME.

1. One reason is that time is so precious in itself.
2. Another reason is that so much of our time is gone.
3. Another reason is, that our hold on what remains is so uncertain.

II. THE GREAT USES FOR WHICH TIME IS TO BE REDEEMED.

1. The sinner is to redeem time for his own salvation.
2. The child of God is to redeem it for building up a Christlike character.
3. The servant of Christ is to redeem time for works of love and helpfulness.

— HOMILETIC LIBRARY.

(SERMON THEMES AND TEXTS)

1. The Irrevocable Past, "Ye shall henceforth return no more that way" (Deut. 17:16).

2. The End Better Than the Beginning, "Better is the end of a thing than the beginning thereof" (Eccl. 7:8).
3. A Trustworthy Leader, "And he led them on safely, so that they feared not" (Ps. 75:53).
4. God's Purpose, He brought thee out — to bring thee in" (Deut. 4:37, 38).

THE LOG BOOK OF THE YEAR

Life is styled a voyage over the ocean of Time to the harbor haven of Eternity. The last daily account of the Log Book on Columbus' celebrated voyage reads, "Sailed all this day due west, which was our course." On the last day of the old year, how noble if we could truly write, "Sailed all the day due Heavenward, which was our course." Then at last, when all the years are passed, we shall reach the desired haven.

Are you adrift, floating aimlessly, or on a voyage of discovery seeking a new world?

— REV. CASWELL.

TRIFLING WITH TIME

Every day, every hour in the day, is a talent of time; and God expects the improvement of it, and will charge the non-improvement of it upon you at last.

> Our fathers' God from out whose hand,
> The centuries fall like grains of sand,
> We meet to-day, united, free,
> And loyal to our land and Thee,
> To thank Thee for the era done,
> And trust Thee for the opening one.
>
> — WHITTIER.